Su...

Geraniums and Pelargoniums

ANDREAS RIEDMILLER

Series Editor:
LESLEY YOUNG

MEREHURST

Contents

Contents

Introduction

It is the gardener's dream to gaze from a window at an idyllic view of lovely summer flowers in glowing colours. Try to imagine glorious blooms of red, pink and white - in a window box, on a balcony or on a patio - and you will find you have conjured up a vision of luxuriantly blooming geraniums. For generations geraniums have been some of the most popular flowering plants for tubs and baskets. The gardener who looks after them, waters them diligently and fusses over them, will have only one aim: to encourage them to continue to produce flowers endlessly. This guide will help you to buy and grow healthy plants that will later produce a mass of beautiful flowers.

One important point must be made right from the start. Few people are aware that the plant that most of us call "geranium" is, correctly speaking, a pelargonium. The real geranium, on the other hand, is actually a hardy garden shrub which looks quite different to a pelargonium. This guide will introduce you to the splendid range of colours and the enormous selection of pelargonium varieties and species with the help of over a hundred colour photographs and detailed individual descriptions. Among these are some new varieties of exotic wild, scented-leaved, fancy-leaved and regal pelargoniums for indoors. Many of the beautiful photographs were specially taken by the author himself. You will be introduced to the sculpted leaves and orchid-like flowers of the wild and scented-leaved pelargoniums and to the vibrant colours of the regal pelargoniums. You will also learn new and often surprising facts about the uni-versally popular balcony pelargoniums. Did you know, for example, that these popular flowers are really subtropical plants that originated in the dry, hot areas of South Africa? For this reason alone, their special requirements with respect to care must be observed. In this guide, Andreas Riedmiller provides a sound, basic knowledge of these plants in brief, easy-to-understand terms, and shares with the reader his gardening secrets so that your plants will flourish and flower more abundantly than ever.

Drawing on his own experience, he supplies detailed instructions on buying, care and propagating. Colour illustrations, with step-by-step explanations, supplement his excellent text. Advice on how to make your own potting compost, basic and regular feeding and the use of the right plant containers backs up the mass of expert information. A section on problems, pests and diseases will help to pre-vent such troubles and direct you towards the right treatment if diffi-culties do arise. If you wish to keep your beloved pelargoniums for more than one season, you will find advice on what to do in the chapter on overwintering, which covers var-ious methods of nursing your pelargoniums through the dormant period. The chapter on propagating offers an alternative for those who wish to produce new plants for the following year, either from seeds or cuttings.

Note
In order to help you to find your way through this book more easily, each chapter has been divided into three sections, based on the posi-tion in which the pelargoniums will be kept, both indoors and outside:
- upright, hanging and semi-pen-dent pelargoniums for balconies and patios;
- pelargoniums for indoors;
- geraniums for the garden.

The author
Andreas Riedmiller was born in 1952. He trained to be a gardener, specializing in the growing of flow-ering and ornamental plants, and then worked as a specialist advisor to garden centres for ten years before becoming the manager of a garden centre. At present, he is a freelance photographer. The main emphasis of his work is now on ecological and biological topics and on landscape, nature and plant photography. His publications include a guide to trees, and he has made numerous contributions to specialist and popular periodi-cals, books and calendars.

Acknowledgements
The author and publishers wish to thank all those who contributed towards this volume, especially György Jankovics for his excellent colour illustrations and the author's wife, Uschi Riedmiller, for all her help and co-operation in the com-piling of the text. Special thanks go to Mrs Wiedemann of Geislingen-Aufhausen, to Mr Gibboni at the firm of Pelargonien Fischer and to Mr Leinfelder at the Garden Research Centre in Weihenstephan for permission to photograph rare and especially splendid varieties.

Prized flowering plants
Pelargoniums – here a hanging cascade variety – displaying their beauty in a sun-drenched garden.

All about geraniums and pelargoniums

Geraniums and pelargoniums are two completely different groups of plants whose names are used incorrectly and interchangeably all the time. This chapter will explain the differences between geraniums and pelargoniums and will give some interesting information on each group.

Naming and classification

When the first pelargoniums were brought by merchants from South Africa to Europe, around 1700, they were called *Geranium* and, even though the French botanist Charles-Louis I'Hertier de Brutelle eventually placed them among the pelargoniums in 1789, to this day, the popular but incorrect designation "geranium" has persisted in the English-speaking world. Pelargoniums are among the most popular of all balcony and window-box plants and are so easy to look after that one tends to assume automatically that discovering the names of different varieties might be just as easy. Alas, this is not the case and it is for this reason that I wish to begin by explaining the names and terms so that you will find it a little easier to choose your plants.

Although specialist pelargonium growers and plant nurseries or garden centres usually give the correct terms in their lists and catalogues, you will still often find them incorrectly described in flower shops and on stalls in markets, etc.

Pelargoniums

Whether their owners call them geraniums or pelargoniums, the plants that you see flowering in glorious shades of red on balconies, hanging luxuriantly from window-boxes or flourishing on patios, are really pelargoniums. Right from the start, in order to avoid confusion, I shall call these plants by their proper name – pelargonium – throughout this book.

Wild pelargoniums

One thing that you may not know is that the pelargoniums that we like to grow in our windowboxes and on balconies and patios are nothing like the plants that arrived in Europe for the first time around 1700. Those plants that were introduced from the Cape in South Africa were wild plants with much smaller flowers (see photos p. 53), much smaller umbels and, very often, smaller leaves too. Wild pelargoniums still grow in South Africa today, forming bushes up to 2 m (6½ ft) high. Today, wild pelargoniums are enjoying increasing popularity all over the world and are grown alongside hybridized

pelargoniums. They are cultivated both as indoor pot plants and as summer plants outside. Their delicate flowers may sometimes resemble orchids, and the leaves of many species release a pleasant scent.

Scented-leaved pelargoniums are much sought after. Most are wild pelargoniums with scented leaves, but some are hybrid crosses of different scented-leaved species (see p. 50).

Hybrids

"Hybrid" is the correct term for a plant that has been created through crossing different species – sometimes called a "bastard cross". Except for the wild ones, all pelargoniums are hybrids, which makes them all the results of human interference. There are very many of these hybrids, which can be divided into five different groups.

My tip: You can recognize wild pelargoniums and hybrids by the way their botanical name is written: in the case of wild pelargoniums the genus name (the first name) is written with an uppercase (capital) letter and the species name has a lowercase (small) first letter. Hybrid names are written with uppercase letters for both names.

Zonal pelargoniums are hybrids that were created by crossing the *Pelargonium zonale* and the *Pelargonium inquinans* (see p. 8). They are also called "upright pelargoniums". The name zonal refers to the brownish ring (*zonale* = *girdle*) on the leaves (see p. 47). *Hanging pelargoniums* (properly, *Pelargonium – Peltatum hybrids*) are the result of crossing *Pelargonium peltatum* and other wild pelargoniums. These are also called, "ivy-leaved pelargoniums" or

Hanging pelargoniums, especially the cascade varieties, are most prolific, producing a mass of blooms.

"shield pelargoniums" (see photos p. 49).

Semi-pendent pelargoniums
(properly, *Pelargonium – Zonale* x *Peltatum* hybrids) were created by crossing two hybrids: the zonal and hanging hybrids. They are also called semi-hanging or semi-peltate pelargoniums (photo No. 5, p. 49).

Fancy-leaved pelargoniums
belong, for the most part, among the zonal pelargoniums. However, some of them are also hanging hybrids. Mutations of their genetic composition have resulted in espe-cially interesting leaf shapes and leaf markings. These pelargoniums are now being hybridized to per-petuate these characteristics, although they also possess beauti-ful flowers. (photos p. 57).

Regal pelargoniums (properly, *Pelargonium – Grandiflorum* hybrids) are derived from *Pelargonium cucullatum* and other wild species. They are also some-times called "indoor pelargoniums" (photos p. 55).

The naming of pelargoniums
This is occasionally a confusing business. Over the years, all of the above-named hybrids have been the subject of hybridizing to pro-duce hundreds of varieties of pelargoniums. It can prove very dif-ficult for the amateur pelargonium grower to distinguish between plants which look very alike, espe-cially in photographs, when new varieties seem to appear all the time.

The ancestors of all zonal pelargonium hybrids
Left: Pelargonium zonale. Right: Pelargonium inquinans.

How to distinguish pelargoniums from geraniums

Together with other genera, the two genera *Pelargonium* and *Geranium* belong to the family, or natural order, of plants called *Geraniaceae.* In addition to other characteristics, pelargoniums and geraniums may be distinguished quite easily by their flowers and fruits.
Pelargonium means "stork's bill" (Greek: *pelargos* = stork), which refers to the shape of the long fruits. The flowers may be divided into two symmetrical halves (zygomorph) and they have a nectary.
Geranium means "crane's bill" (Greek: geranos = crane). This name also refers to the shape of the fruits, which are split and are a little shorter than those of the pelargonium. The flowers are regular, radial and have no nectary.

Pelargoniums as medicinal plants

The South African peoples use the roots and other parts of pelargonium plants for medicinal purposes. The crushed stalks of one species serve as a remedy for headaches and as a perfume or body lotion, while other species yield leaves which can be dried and smoked like tobacco leaves. In southern Europe, some species of pelargonium, such as *Pelargonium radens* or *Pelargonium graveolens*, are grown for the subsequent extraction of geraniol (geranium oil), which is one of the basic substances used in perfume manufacturing. Other healing properties of the wild pelargonium are still largely unknown to the western world, and this plant may well yield other useful natural substances in the future.

However, a word of caution is due here: a new name does not necessarily signify a new hybrid. Some gardening catalogues may try to "freshen up" old favourites by giving them new, fanciful names every year. The lists on pages 44-57 are designed to help you when buying pelargoniums.

My tip: Do not become confused if you come across yet another new term, namely pelargonium F₁ hybrids. "F" is the abbreviation for Latin *"filia"*, meaning daughter, and "F₁" designates the first daughter generation of a particular cross. F₁ hybrids are of special interest to the gardener, as they can be propagated from seed (see p. 32) unlike all other pelargonium hybrids which can only be propagated from cuttings (see p. 35).

Geraniums

Geraniums are perennial, hardy shrubs that flower from late spring to early autumn and are very undemanding. The parts of the plant above ground will die down every autumn. Geraniums need no extra protection through the winter. In spring, they will put out new shoots.
Wild types: The wild varieties of geraniums are especially at home in the Pyrenees, the Caucasus Mountains and Asia, where they still grow wild.
Hybrids: In gardens and garden centres you will usually find cultivated geranium hybrids, which can grow from 10 cm (4 in) to 1 m (40 in) in height, depending on the species. Their flower umbels are white, pink, red, violet or blue (see pp. 58/59).

Where to grow pelargoniums

As a rule, we tend to grow pelargoniums on patios, balconies and indoors, whereas geraniums are only grown in the garden. How to choose the best site for each species or variety is explained in the following sections.

On patios and balconies
Most pelargoniums are kept in windowboxes, on windowsills, on patios or on balconies during the warm, frost-free months of the year. These are usually pelargonium hybrids of the zonal or hanging varieties.

Indoors
Regal, wild, scented-leaved and fancy-leaved pelargoniums will flourish indoors and seem to thrive even in the dry atmosphere of centrally heated rooms. Regal pelargoniums, especially, are often considered to be true house plants because of these characteristics. During the warm part of the year, however, these plants are quite happy to be moved outside, where they will flourish in the sunshine.

In the garden
Geranium hybrids, as already mentioned, are hardy garden shrubs. They develop a widely spreading root system but will thrive equally well in large plant containers. *Pelargonium hybrids and fancy-leaved pelargoniums* can be planted in flowerbeds during the summer months. Because they are not hardy, however, they will not survive frosts and must be moved indoors before these occur.
Note: Depending on their position, pelargoniums and geraniums require different kinds of care, so each chapter of this book is divided to take account of the three main sites.

Wild pelargoniums growing in a typical, arid position in South Africa.

Where to find geraniums and pelargoniums

Not all geraniums and pelargoniums are easy to obtain. Certain rare varieties seem only to be exchanged among specialist enthusiasts and are sought after as veritable treasures. The most usual source for the more common plants, however, will be garden centres or nurseries etc.

The gardening trade
Nurseries: In nurseries, you may choose your pelargoniums from source, right out of the greenhouse. *Flower shops, gardening specialist shops* and *garden centres* also offer opportunities to buy these plants. During the planting season, you will also find a wide range of accessories in these places, such as potting compost, fertilizers and plant containers.
Mail order nurseries also offer pelargoniums in colourful, well-illustrated catalogues. You cannot go to choose your own plants when buying them this way but, on the other hand, you need not transport them yourself either.

Seeds or cuttings
F_1 hybrids (see My tip, p. 8) and wild pelargoniums may be propagated from seeds but all other hybrids are propagated from cuttings only (see p. 35). You can obtain pelargonium seeds through the gardening trade and acquire cuttings, perhaps from accommodating neighbours or friends, or even in garden centres, any time from the middle of winter until the middle of spring.

Fancy-leaved pelargoniums (here the silver-leaved variety, "Chelsea Gem") will thrive indoors or out in summer.

Buying geraniums and pelargoniums

Pelargoniums for patios and balconies

When to buy: You can buy pelargonium hybrid rooted cuttings from the middle of winter through to the middle of spring, as half-grown plants from early spring, and as full-grown plants from late spring.

Rooted cuttings should show compact growth, deep green foliage without any discoloration and have numerous roots, which will protrude from the propagation pot. Rooted cuttings with yellowish leaves which straggle and look unhealthy should be avoided.

Half-grown plants are pelargoniums with one growing shoot, and are sold in pots of about 9 cm (3½ in) in diameter. These plants should show compact growth and have at least one bud that shows a little colour or is in the process of opening.

Grown plants are sold in pots of 11 cm (4¼ in) in diameter. They will always have several shoots and their flowerbuds will be on the point of opening.

Healthy plants: Make sure that the plants display deep green foliage; this is a sign that they have been fed properly. Also take a look at the undersides of the leaves as this is where pests may lurk. Plants with fungal infestations, insects or larvae (see p. 26) or decaying buds or roots should be avoided.

Withered flowers: If one of the flowers on an otherwise healthy plant happens to be withering, do not let this put you off. Once at home, just break off the stalk (see p. 23).

Pelargoniums for indoors
When to buy: Flowering regal pelargoniums, in pots with a diameter of 11 cm (4¼ in), are usually for sale nearly all year round. Scented-leaved pelargoniums and fancy-leaved pelargoniums, on the other hand, can usually only be obtained from spring onwards into summer, at specialist shops. If you wish to buy one of these plants, you will often have to seek out a pelargonium nursery or specialist grower.
Healthy plants: When looking for regal, scented-leaved or fancy-leaved pelargoniums, make sure the foliage is a deep green in colour. Check whether the pelargoniums are infested with pests or diseases (see p. 26). Regal pelargoniums are fairly resistant to pests and white fly seems to be the only insect they are susceptible to (p.26), but they do appear to be extremely sensitive to waterlogging. Take a look at the saucer or tray in which the plant pot is standing. There should be no water in it.

My tip: Be especially critical if the pelargoniums you find on sale are placed near draughty entrances, under artificial light or in rooms that are too dark. The plant will react to these situations with falling buds and yellowing leaves, and will recover very slowly.

Geraniums for the garden
When to buy: You can purchase geraniums from early spring to late mid-autumn in shrub nurseries or garden centres.
Appearance: When you buy the plants, they should have finished shooting. They are usually sold in plastic containers with a diameter of 9 cm (3½ in).

Transporting plants and care before planting

The best methods of transporting plants are as follows:

Pelargoniums for the patio and balcony
Transport your pelargoniums standing upright in deep boxes or fruit crates.
If you are unable to plant the pelargoniums in their proper containers at home right away, you should at least unpack them and stand them in a light, frost-free room, shed or greenhouse. Water them if they require it and air the room often, as this will help to make them resistant to diseases. Do not remove the support sticks from hanging pelargoniums until several weeks after they have been planted in their new container, so that the plants are not accidentally broken.

Pelargoniums for indoors
If you buy flowering pelargoniums in winter, make sure that the plants are wrapped in thick wads of newspaper. Pelargoniums are very sensitive to frost and on no account should they be exposed to the cold winter air for any length of time. Pelargoniums intended for indoors need not be repotted immediately after purchase. The best position for them is a sunny windowsill.

Geraniums for the garden
As shrub geraniums are usually sold in plastic containers, they need not be planted immediately after purchase. Keep them in the garden, never indoors, so that the plants are not subjected to too much warmth and will not begin shooting too soon.

Geraniums add colour to a wild garden (here Geranium meeboldi).

Planting and initial care

Geraniums and pelargoniums are versatile, decorative plants which have long been used to beautify the home and garden. The better you respond to their needs, the more they will flourish. If you pay careful attention to all their requirements right from the start, such as supplying the correct position, soil, nutrients and containers, you will be well rewarded with a rich profusion of flowers.

Pelargoniums on patios and balconies

Pelargoniums provide an easy way of transforming your patio or balcony into a miniature paradise. When the last cold snap of late spring has passed, you can begin to put both home-grown plants and bought pelargoniums outside. Now is the time to take young plants out of their propagating pots and plant them in their final pots.
Providing you offer them all they require in the way of care – the right position, correct feeding, sufficient water and a little attention – your new plants, cuttings and overwintered favourites will respond with strong, healthy growth and a profusion of flowers.

The right position

Before planting, you must give some thought as to the future positioning of your plants. As they originated in a subtropical climate, pelargoniums need lots of sunlight and heat in order to grow properly. For this reason, the position you choose should be sunny or at least semi-sunny. Such conditions will be supplied by windowsills, patios and balconies on the south, south-west or south-east sides of the house.
What the flowers and leaves of pelargoniums really love, of course, is a position in full sunlight. The roots, however, can react adversely to extreme heat. If the sunlight is very intense, therefore, and the plants are in thin-walled balcony boxes (for example, made of plastic), too high a temperature may occur among the roots and thus damage the plant. In order to avoid such problems, give your flower-boxes some protection by fastening a piece of wood along the side that is exposed to the sun. This will help to reduce the detrimental effects of heat on the roots somewhat, and the soil will not dry out so easily either.

Ready-mixed potting compost

General rule: Pelargoniums like medium-heavy soil (that is, a loose mixture of loam, peat and sand) that is well aerated and rich in nutrients and of a fine, crumbly consistency. This type of soil will crumble loosely in one's fingers, feel slightly moist and have a pleasant, earthy smell. A pH of 6.5-7 is best.
Commercial potting composts: You will find a vast range of composts, with different names and of varying quality, in nurseries and garden centres. The differences between products can be very difficult for the layman to figure out. The main ingredient of all these commercial products is peat.
Cheap potting composts: Some of the cheaper composts consist of peat only. Such composts are not suitable for pelargoniums as the nutrients tend to get washed out of peat rather quickly in heavy rain. Furthermore, peat does not aid drainage and will make the compost either too wet or too dry. There is a great danger of the soil remaining wet for too long and pelargonium roots cannot stand being waterlogged. The darker kind of peat (sedge peat) is completely unsuitable for pelargoniums as it is too acid.
Standard potting compost: I recommend a standard potting compost for pelargoniums, with a loam content of at least 30%. The percentage of loam should always be indicated on the packaging of standard potting composts. This is more expensive than some other commercial composts but, due to its percentage of loam, it will retain nutrients much longer and ensure that the plants receive an adequate supply of water. Standard potting composts also contain a high per-

Pelargoniums will flourish in a sunny position and contribute colour and vibrancy to their surroundings.

centage of nutrients, which means that you will not need to give your pelargoniums an initial feed of fertilizer, as you would when using other commercial composts.

Mixing your own potting compost

This is recommended if you already have some kind of soil at your disposal, whether it is humus or garden compost, or compost left over from the previous year.

Method 1 – using leftover compost as a base

If you have decided that you do not wish to, or cannot, overwinter your pelargonium plants but would like to grow pelargoniums next year, you might wish to try this.
Important: On no account should you re-use the soil of diseased plants – throw it away! Never overwinter sick plants (see p. 28)!
Procedure: In late autumn, cut off all the shoots above ground.
● Use polythene to cover up the plant containers, in order to retain

sufficient moisture in the soil.
● Place the plant containers in a frost-free position for the winter. The finer roots will have completely decayed by the following spring.
● Before planting the new pelargoniums in spring, empty the old flowerpots, remove the old rootstocks, then loosen the earth with your fingers. You should now have pure compost again. If there is not enough, you will be able to mix in bought, standard potting compost.
● This re-used potting compost will need initial fertilizing (see p. 15).

13

Stay green: If you have a balcony or live in a town, you may be able to do your bit to protect the environment. As commercial potting composts consist mainly of peat, their use in gardening is leading to considerable detrimental pressure on our natural wetlands. For this reason, you should always be very conscious of how you use bought potting compost and try to conserve it whenever you can. Do not, however, keep any compost that has been in contact with diseased plants!

Method 2 – using humus as a base

Pure humus (the top, usually dark brown, layer of soil) or agricultural soil is too heavy for pelargoniums. *Procedure:* Mix equal amounts of humus with rotted-down leaf mould or, at a pinch, peat. In order to avoid the growth of weeds, try to eliminate all grass sods and roots. This mixture of soil will need to be mixed again with a fertilizer.

Method 3 – using composting soil as a base

If you are lucky enough to be the owner of a compost heap, you should have exactly the right type of soil for your pelargoniums. Not only is garden compost full of nutrients, it also contains many micro-organisms that are capable of transforming organic substances into nutrients required by plants. *Procedure:* Simply pass the well-mixed compost through a wide-mesh sieve and then mix in a little lime. In this way, the nutrients that are abundantly present in the compost will be made accessible to the plant. Such compost will contain so many essential nutrients that you need not give your plants any initial fertilizer.

△ *Zonal pelargoniums, variety "Casino".*
▽ *Zonal pelargonium "Kardinal" is suitable for flowerbeds too.*

Feeding

Pelargoniums require the major nutrients of nitrogen (N), phosphorous (P) and potassium (K) for continuous growth and a profusion of flowers. In addition, they will also need small amounts of other substances (for example, magnesium, iron, sulphur, manganese, boron, copper, etc.). These are called trace elements. The simplest way to give nutrients to your pelargoniums is in doses of fertilizer. Fertilizers that contain all main nutrients are called compound fertilizers.

General rule: The correct initial fertilizer for pelargoniums is a compound fertilizer in a dry, granulated form, which is mixed with soil or compost.

Compound fertilizers

You can obtain compound fertilizers in a dry, granulated form (especially suitable for initial fertilizing) or as a liquid which is dissolved in water (especially recommended for the regular fertilizing of pelargoniums, see p. 22). There should be information about the nutrient content, the "N-P-K" ratio on the packaging. This may appear simply as a sequence of numbers, and indicates the percentages of each nutrient. For example: 15-11-15 means 15% nitrogen, 11% phosphorous and 15% potassium. If this kind of triple ratio is given on the packet, this will tell you that it is a compound fertilizer.

Compound fertilizers are not only distinguished by the form in which they are sold (bulk or liquid), but also by the way in which the main nutrients are bound to certain substances.

Inorganic (mineral) compound fertilizers: The best known representative of this type is a fertilizer which looks like small blue granules (such as lawn fertilizer). The nutrients and trace elements in inorganic fertilizers are bound to synthetic substances – for example, salts. In the case of bulk inorganic compound fertilizers, the nutrients are dissolved by moisture (for example, during watering or rainfall), while the nutrients are already dissolved in liquid, inorganic compound fertilizers. In both cases the plant can absorb the nutrients directly.

● Advantage: fertilizing action commences immediately.

● Disadvantage: too much moisture (for example, during long periods of wet weather) may cause the nutrients to be washed out rather quickly. This is something you must watch out for: if you use too much fertilizer, the soil may accumulate salts which may then burn the roots and leaves.

Organic-mineral compound fertilizers: These are fertilizers in which the nutrients nitrogen (N) and phosphorous (P) are bound to organic substances. (These can be animal products, such as horn meal, horn chips, bone meal, fish meal, dried blood, guano and so on.) Potassium, on the other hand, is usually bound to inorganic substances. If you use one of these fertilizers on your pelargoniums, a very different process will be activated to the one that occurs with inorganic fertilizers. The plant is unable to absorb organically bound nutrients directly. The nutrients must first be broken down and transformed by soil-dwelling micro-organisms and bacteria. Incredible as it sounds, one handful of soil can harbour more of these micro-organisms than there are human beings living on this planet! During this transformation process, all the basic building materials needed by the plant for growth (for example, nitrogen, phosphorous and so on) are released and can then be absorbed by the plant in the form of inorganic substances. This is called mineralization.

● Advantages: If you use a fertilizer with organic components, the activity of micro-organisms and bacteria in the soil is stimulated, more humus is created and the soil will become more fertile. Furthermore, the soil will not become saturated with salts (as it can do with inorganic fertilizers) and the fertilizing effect will last longer. Organic-mineral fertilizers comprise natural, basic substances and are, therefore, environmentally friendly!

● Disadvantage: As the nutrients must be transformed before they become accessible to the plants, the fertilizing action cannot begin immediately.

Organic (biological) fertilizers: Purely organic fertilizers are very often not compound fertilizers. Usually they will lack the essential plant nutrient of potassium which occurs mainly in inorganic compounds. In the gardening trade organic fertilizers are sold in the form of horn meal, horn chips, bone meal, dried blood, guano, manure and so on. Most of these fertilizers yield only one nutrient each; for example, horn chips provide nitrogen, bone meal provides phosphorous. Initial fertilizing should, therefore, include a mixture of different fertilizers containing different nutrients. These are sold in the trade as "bio-fertilizers" and can also be called compound fertilizers if they contain potassium too.

Initial fertilizing

General rule: Any soil in which you intend to plant pelargoniums – with the exception of garden compost and standard potting compost which already contain nutrients – should have a good bulk compound fertilizer mixed in with it.

The following are the two most useful methods of basic fertilizing:

Method 1 – basic fertilizing with organic minerals: There is a large range of ready-made organic-mineral compound fertilizers to choose from in the gardening trade. For a basic fertilizer, use a bulk compound fertilizer with a higher than usual percentage of nitrogen, as nitrogen encourages the growth of stalks and leaves (table, p. 22) and will strengthen your young plants. One alternative would be a bio-fertilizer (also a purely organic fertilizer mixture) but, again, make sure to use a bulk fertilizer containing a high percentage of nitrogen.

● Use the proper dosage! The correct ratio of fertilizer to soil to be used is usually written on the fertilizer packaging. If there is no indication, stick to an average value of a maximum of 70 g (2 oz) of organic-mineral fertilizer to 10 litres (2 gal) of soil. In a bio-fertilizer the nutrients are less concentrated than in ready-made organic-mineral or inorganic fertilizer mixes. This means that you will hardly ever run the risk of overfeeding your plants. Nevertheless, still make sure to consult the dosage instructions on the packaging of bio-fertilizers.

● Distribute the fertilizer thoroughly! Make sure the compound fertilizer is mixed in evenly with the soil. The best way to do this is to sprinkle the bulk compound fertilizer on to the soil and turn it over several times with a spade.

● Note how long the stock of nutrients will last. Organic-mineral compound fertilizers will supply the soil with about six weeks' worth of all essential nutrients, although this is only an approximate estimation. Note the date of application and then repeat the dose after six weeks, using a liquid compound fertilizer (with a higher phosphorous content which favours the development of flowers) when you water (see regular feeding, p. 22).

Method 2 – controlled-release fertilizers as an alternative
Controlled-release fertilizers are inorganic compound fertilizers. They comprise small granules in which the nutrients are captured in a highly concentrated form. When the granules are moistened, they become permeable and continuously release a nutrient solution.

● Use the correct dose! Keep strictly to the quantities recommended on the packaging so that your plants do not suffer from a build up of salts in the soil (see inorganic fertilizer, p. 15). If the quantities are not indicated, use the following as a guide: use 1 tbsp per plant or 5 tbsp for a flowerbox measuring about 80 cm (32 in) in length.

● Mix thoroughly! Stir the controlled-release fertilizer into the soil so that it is evenly distributed.

● Note how long the nutrient supply will last. Controlled-release fertilizers will provide plants with nutrients over a period of three to four months, and represent an alternative to organic-mineral fertilizing.

Important: It would be wrong to assume that the above method of fertilizing means that you need not be concerned with supplying nutrients to your plants for the next three months of the year. A period of heavy rain, for example, will cause nutrients to be released and washed out more quickly, so that the fertilizing process will be over sooner than planned and will usually stop rather suddenly. You will then notice that the foliage of your pelargoniums is beginning to turn yellow. If this happens, use an inorganic liquid fertilizer when watering (see regular feeding, p. 22), or sprinkle a fast-working, bulk inorganic fertilizer (for example, the blue-granule type, obtainable at garden centres) on to the damp soil.

Plant containers

Pelargoniums may be planted in a variety of containers, for example flowerboxes on window ledges or balconies. Plastic boxes are very useful. They mostly come in two widths (15 cm or 6 in and 20 cm or 8 in), and varying lengths. They are not heavy, are easy to transport and are strong and stable. However, you need not be restricted to boxes: pelargoniums will thrive happily in pots, basins, hanging baskets, amphorae, even in old sinks. On the whole, the material out of which the container is made should have no effect whatever on the growth of your plants, although you should make sure that the container does not contain oxidizing substances like copper, tin or zinc, as these would have a detrimental, or even toxic, effect on your plants.

Choosing plant containers

● Pelargonium roots cannot tolerate waterlogging. Whatever type of container you choose, it must have drainage holes.

● Pelargoniums can develop into magnificent bushes of considerable width. Your containers should, therefore, be very stable so that they will not tip over at the first strong gust of wind.

● The pelargonium will need enough room to spread out its roots and develop properly. If you choose the wider type of balcony box (20 cm or 8 in), your plants will reward you with an extra-abundant crop of flowers.

● Pelargoniums that are kept in boxes fixed to balcony railings should have suitable trays or other arrangements for catching drainage water and adjustable, strong balcony fixtures (those made of metal are best). Both of these items are obtainable from garden centres etc.

● Hanging containers should be made of lightweight materials (for example, plastic); this makes them easier to transport and puts less of a strain on the fixtures.

● Only containers that are definitely frost-proof can be kept outside in the winter (for example, containers made of plastic). Clay pots are especially sensitive in freezing temperatures and may then crack or flake.

My tip: Containers that taper conically downwards provide less surface area for frost attack and are, therefore, more frost-resistant.

Tips on preparing plant containers

New clay pots: New clay pots should be prepared for use by immersing them completely in water until you can no longer see any tiny air bubbles rising to the surface. This soaking will remove any production residue still adhering to the pot and will also prevent a very dry pot from depriving the soil of moisture by drawing it out.

How to use your plants artistically
Zonal and hanging pelargoniums in balcony boxes in combination with other summer flowers and in hanging baskets.

17

Used containers: Any residue of any kind should be rinsed off thoroughly. Use clean water for this purpose. Pots which have had diseased plants in them should be treated with disinfectant which, in turn, should be well rinsed.

Drainage holes: All pots will need workable drainage holes so that there will be no waterlogging. Do not forget to pierce the pre-marked holes in some new flowerboxes.

Protecting the drainage holes: Before filling a flowerpot with soil, place a piece of broken pot, with the curved side up, over the drainage holes, to prevent the earth from clogging the holes. In the case of very large containers, it is a good idea to place an entire layer of pot shards or Hortag (a lightweight expanded clay aggregate) in the bottom of the pot.

Segregating layer: Over the top of the drainage layer, lay a piece of fabric which will prevent the soil from penetrating the drainage layer. This arrangement will help surplus water to drain away easily. Hortag stores moisture and will serve as a small water reservoir.

Filling in the compost: Now fill the pot with compost up to 2 cm (¾ in) below the top of the pot. To make things easier, stand all the pots close together to avoid spilling compost over the edges.

How to plant correctly

● Water the pelargoniums a few hours before planting them, so that their rootstocks will not be dry. Then line up the plants on your work table in the sequence of planting.

● To remove the plant from its pot, gently grasp the top of the rootstock between your second and third fingers (see illustration), turn the pot upside down and lightly tap the rim of the pot against the edge of the table. The pot can then be removed quite easily, and without damaging the rootstock, by giving a slight twist. On no account should you remove the latticed netting used for propagating, through which the roots have grown (see p. 34).

● Make a depression in the soil and stand the rootstock in it so that the top edges of the roots are no deeper down than they were in the propagating pot.

● Using your hand, press the soil down all around the rootstock so that contact with the roots is ensured.

● Do not plant more than five pelargoniums in a box measuring 1 m (40 in) long.

● Make sure that hanging pelargoniums are planted leaning forwards slightly.

● When all the pelargoniums have been planted, a gap of 1 cm (¼ in) must be left all round at the top of

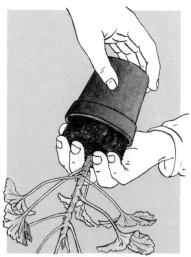

Removing a plant from its pot
Grasp the rootstock between your second and third fingers, turn the pot upside down and twist slightly with the other hand.

the box so that watering will not cause soil to be washed away.

Initial care

The newly planted pelargoniums should now be placed in their final position and watered gently so that the soil is not washed away. Check them over once more before leaving them:

● If leaves or flowers have snapped off during replanting or transportation to their new site, you should remove them now.

● If the pelargoniums are left standing under some kind of cover, they will be protected from rain and storms. Alternatively, you can buy polythene hoods to act as a protection against strong winds, rain and hail. These hoods are also very useful during long periods of incessant rain and will prevent constant wetness around the roots, which might cause them to decay.

Indoor pelargoniums

The best position
Regal, scented-leaved and fancy-leaved pelargoniums prefer direct sunlight, so you should place them near a south-facing window which can be shaded during periods of strong sunlight.

The right soil
Pelargoniums that are destined for indoors need not be repotted immediately after purchasing and will, therefore, not need new soil.

Initial fertilizing
This will be necessary as a basic fertilizing should always accompany repotting in new soil or compost.

Plant pots
Pelargoniums for indoors can

remain in the pot in which they were originally bought.

They should only be planted in a larger pot when the old one is too small (see p. 25). A pot is too small if the roots have used up all the soil and now fill the entire pot. This is not necessarily what has happened if you see roots hanging out of the drainage holes. If you think it is time for the plant to be repotted, remove it from its pot (see p. 18) and check how much room the roots still have in the old pot.

Plants kept indoors look particularly attractive in a decorative pot holder. There should be a gap of 1.5 cm (⅜ in) between the inner and outer pots as this makes for better circulation of air around the plant pot. If you do place your indoor pelargoniums in pot holders, make sure, when you water them, that no surplus water remains in the bottom of the pot holder, which could cause the roots to decay.

Pelargoniums ("Feuercascade") in a hanging basket on a pergola.

Geraniums in the garden

The best position

Shrub geraniums prefer to be in a half-shady position, for example, between high grasses or other shrubs.

The right soil

As shrub geraniums favour a nutrient-rich soil, the best soil for them should contain humus or loam.

Initial fertilizing

Give each individual shrub geranium a handful of bio-fertilizer by sprinkling it into the soil when you plant. This will be sufficient to stimulate plant growth and produce lots of flowers.

Planting

You will nearly always buy shrub geraniums as container plants which can then be planted out at any time during the entire growing season. Occasionally, you may be able to obtain them as half-grown cuttings and then the right time to plant is early spring (shortly after the plant has begun to shoot) or in the autumn (after the geranium has died back and the leaves and stalks have turned brown).

Method

● With a spade, dig a hole (about 30 x 30 cm or 12 x 12 in) and mix the soil you have removed with a handful of bio-fertilizer.

● Fill up the hole again with half of the mixture.

● Carefully remove the shrub geranium from its container and use one hand to hold the top of the roots against the top of the soil because the geranium should not be planted any deeper in the soil than it was in its original container.

● With the other hand distribute the rest of the soil-fertilizer mixture around the rootstock and press it down lightly.

● Finally, water thoroughly so that the soil envelopes the rootstock.

Initial care

If the weather is very dry after planting, you will need to water your shrub geranium occasionally. After a fortnight, it should be established and further watering will not be necessary as the normal amount of rain should generally be sufficient.

Successful care – simple but vital

Giving pelargoniums and geraniums the best care during the summer means, above all, supplying them with the proper amounts of water and nutrients. In addition, there are also other duties, such as removing withered leaves or flowers, shortening shoots that have grown too long, removing weeds and taking preventive measures to avoid and combat pests and diseases.

Pelargoniums on balconies and patios

Now that you have planted your pelargoniums with loving care, you will be able to look forward to the day when they will develop a mass of brilliantly coloured blooms. Very little care is required for this, as pelargoniums are easy to look after and will reward you for just a little care with a lavish display of bright flowers.

Watering

Pelargoniums love the sun and will not mind drying out completely very occasionally as they are able to store moisture in their fleshy stalks and leaves. In this way they are able to survive long dry periods in their country of origin without coming to any harm. Too much moisture, on the other hand, will quickly lead to rotting roots. Proper watering is extremely important for pelargoniums.

My tip: Pelargoniums in small containers will need watering more often than plants in windowboxes.

When and how often to water

General rule: Do not water until the soil is really dry – but then do it thoroughly. A mere glance at the soil will not be sufficient; you will have to give the soil a prod with your finger to check whether it is still damp. If it is, it is probably better not to water.

On hot summer days the soil will dry out quickly and, for that reason, you should water the plants daily (in the case of small containers, perhaps even twice daily), preferably in the early evening and/or early in the morning, as less water will evaporate then than during the heat of the day.

On cool, rainy days check the soil thoroughly and, if damp, do not water, as continuous wetness can lead to root damage within six hours.

Occasionally, on rainy days, pelargoniums that are kept under a cover may be forgotten. You may simply have assumed that all the plants will be watered by the rain, without thinking about their position. Be sure to check all your pelargoniums, even during long periods of rain, and water them if necessary.

Distress signals: Zonal pelargoniums will display leaves that have dried up and hang limply when they are overdue for watering. Hanging pelargoniums will have pale, dried-up leaves, even though they are not withered.

My tip: When watering, remember that pelargoniums are stimulated to develop flowers by receiving lots of sunlight and plenty of heat but relatively little water.

What kind of water to use

Pelargoniums are not sensitive to hard water, so you can use ordinary mains water as well as rain water.

Exception: If you have used a controlled-release fertilizer for the initial feed, you should then only use mains water as rain water will not activate the fertilization process.

How to water

Make sure the water is directed straight on to the soil without wetting the pelargonium's leaves in the process. This will require some care but will prevent an outbreak of fungal disease on the leaves.

Regal pelargonium
This pure white cultivar "Virginia" has especially large umbels.

Watering while you are away

Very often kind friends and neighbours are prepared to take on the task of watering plants while you are away on holiday. Make sure to leave exact instructions for the appropriate care of the pelargoniums on your windowsill, balcony or patio. If there is nobody to help out, you may wish to try out one of various automatic or semi-automatic irrigation systems:

Irrigation system for brief periods of absence: For a short absence, containers of water, which will supply your plants with moisture via a woollen strand or a wick inserted into the soil, may be sufficient. Before going away you really ought to find out how long the water supply will last. In my experience, this method of supplying water cannot be controlled. A thick woollen strand will conduct too much water into the soil for pelargoniums, which will result in persistent wetness and lead to root damage. Before going away, test the thickness of strand needed to supply your plants with the right amount of water.

An alternative method is the use of clay cones (obtainable through the gardening trade) which are inserted into the soil. These cones are connected to an adequate supply of water via a piece of string, wool or a wick. As the clay has a tendency to absorb a certain amount of moisture, it will soak up water through the line and pass it on to the soil.

Irrigation system for a lengthy absence: If you intend to go away for a longish period of time, a droplet irrigation system (obtainable through the gardening trade) may serve well. This can also be purchased as a DIY kit which you can set up yourself. Make sure you get all the necessary information on the working and safety of this installation and check that it works properly before you leave in order to avoid unpleasant surprises on your return.

Regular fertilizing

When planting, you should have given an initial feed of fertilizer (see p. 15) containing nutrients that will be used up after about six weeks.

You will recognize the deficiency symptoms when the plant stops flowering so well and the leaves become smaller and yellowish. If you do nothing at this point, your pelargoniums will soon deteriorate and die. Do not allow matters to reach this point and remember to feed your pelargoniums regularly!

When and how to feed
General rule: Give your plants a liquid compound fertilizer in water once a week (see p. 15), and they will flourish.
It is a simple matter to calculate the correct dosage of liquid fertilizer – you need only follow the instructions on the packet. This should completely eliminate the chance of over- or underfeeding during regular fertilizing, and there will be no danger of the leaves burning through too much fertilizing

Compound fertilizers
Every compound fertilizer contains all the essential nutrients for plant growth (nitrogen, phosphorous and potassium) along with trace elements (see p. 15). The effect of each nutrient on the plant is described in the table below.

The effects of nutrients

Nutrient	Positive effect	Negative effect if dosage too high	Source
nitrogen (N)	encourages growth of all green parts of plant (leaves, stalks, etc.)	oversized, bloated leaves, susceptibility to disease, fewer flowers, weak plant tissue, tendency for shoots to rot	in compound fertilizers, special fertilizers containing, nitrogen, horn products, horn chips, dried blood
phosphorous (P)	encourages development of flowers and seeds	dark green to blue green foliage	in compound fertilizers, "flower" fertilizers, guano, bone meal
potassium (K)	strengthens plant tissue, serves to toughen up and develop seeds	weak plant tissue, leaves that break easily, small seeds	in compound fertilizers, special potassium-rich fertilizers

Breaking off dead flowers
Break them off downwards, close to the axil.

The plant will absorb nutrients according to the law of minimum content; that is, the absorption of all minerals is affected by whatever substance is missing. Therefore, a large amount of nitrogen cannot be absorbed by the plant if phosphorous is missing. For the gardener at home, this means that all nutrients must be given in a balanced ratio – and a compound fertilizer will always contain the right mixture. For regular feeding of pelargoniums you should use a compound fertilizer with a higher content of phosphorous as this promotes the development of lots of flowers. Compound fertilizers with a high phosphorous content are sold in the trade as "flowering" fertilizers. There are also other compound fertilizers among the "special" fertilizers, which are suitable for regular feeding. These fertilizers have been specially formulated to suit the requirements of a particular genus or group of plants. Ask about these at your local garden centre or nursery. The type made especially for balcony plants is ideal for feeding regularly to pelargoniums.

Single-nutrient fertilizer to treat symptoms of deficiency
In addition to the various types of compound fertilizer, there are some fertilizers that contain only one nutrient. These fertilizers should only be used if you notice symptoms of a deficiency in your pelargoniums, which can definitely be traced back to a lack of one particular nutrient.

Further care

Besides watering and feeding, pelargoniums will also need some tidying. This can be done quite easily at the same time as watering.
● Dried up or yellow leaves can be broken off at the axils. The same goes for withered flower stalks (illustration). This will help to prevent diseases from developing in the dead parts and the plants will also look tidier.
● Extra-long shoots (which occur quite often in zonal pelargoniums and stick out beyond the plant) can be cut off – a measure that will help the pelargonium to grow more compactly.
● Weeds in pots or balcony boxes should be pulled out as soon as possible as they will divert nutrients from the pelargoniums.
● Check your plants every so often for diseases or parasites (see pests, p. 26). Carefully turn over a leaf and look underneath it to see if there is any sign of pests. Often aphids or other harmful insects will be found on softer, younger shoots.
● During longer periods of wet weather, your pelargoniums may begin to lose their beautiful appearance. Protect them against the rain with polythene hoods (obtainable through the gardening trade). This will also prevent the roots from decaying and the nutrients from being washed out of the soil.

Indoor pelargoniums

Just like their outdoor relatives, pelargoniums that are kept indoors – such as regal, scented-leaved, wild and fancy-leaved pelargoniums – need lots of light. They will thrive especially well in a bright window position, in direct sunlight and with some means of ventilation. Fancy-leaved pelargoniums are the only ones that can tolerate semi-shady positions, however too much shade will cause them to lose their interesting leaf markings and the leaves will turn pure green. Dry indoor air will not harm your pelargoniums at all as the wild species which produced their ancestors live in very dry or desert-like regions and are used to drought. During the summer they will flourish outdoors in a position that is protected from too much rain.
Watering: Water all indoor pelargoniums sparingly. The soil should never be completely moist. The regal pelargonium will react most sensitively to too much water. If its soil becomes too moist, it will develop yellow leaves and the buds will die. If this should happen, allow the soil to dry out and the plant will recover again after a while.

Pelargonium odoratissimum

"White Unique" (hybrid)

Pelargonium tomentosum

Pelargonium quercifolium

"Joy Lucile" (hybrid)

Pelargonium viscosissimum

Pelargonium graveolens

Pelargonium radens

Pelargonium glutinosum

Regular feeding: Regal and fancy-leaved pelargoniums should be given a liquid compound fertilizer once a week, containing a high percentage of phosphorous (for example, a "flowering" or "balcony" fertilizer). Make sure you follow the dosage instructions on the packaging. Scented-leaved pelargoniums are usually a pure wild variety and should be fertilized only sparingly. They, too, should receive a liquid compound fertilizer with a high percentage of phosphorous, but only once a fortnight and only half the dose suggested on the packaging. If they are given too much fertilizer, these delicate plants will lose their original shape and their leaves and shoots will become unnaturally large. Stop feeding them just before the winter rest period (for fancy-leaved pelargoniums, early autumn, for regal and scented-leaved pelargoniums, the second month of winter, see p. 31), so that the plants can rest. Do not start feeding them again until the early part of spring.

Flowers and old leaves should be snapped off and removed in the same way as with outdoor pelargoniums (illustration, p. 23).

Repotting: The regal pelargonium, in particular, can develop into a vigorous bush which will need a new pot every year.

Scented-leaved and wild pelargonium leaves
A wealth of shapes, beautifully formed and usually with a pleasant scent which is released when the fine, scent-bearing hairs are touched.

● The proper time to repot is before the beginning of a new vegetation period (around early to mid-spring) or after the first flowering phase (around the second or third month of summer).
● For this purpose it is best to use a new clay pot which you have soaked well beforehand (p. 17). The new pot should always be 2 cm (¾ in) larger than the old one.
● The best potting compost is the standard kind, which you should mix with a little sand as the soil is already fertilized. If using a home-made compost, you may need to mix in a bulk organic-mineral compound fertilizer (see basic fertilizing, p. 15).

Checking growth: Vigorously growing pelargoniums should be cut back a little from time to time (illustration, p. 30). Use a sharp knife or a pair of scissors to cut off the top shoots of the pelargonium. The dormant leaf buds in the remaining leaf axils will now start to develop into new shoots. This, in turn, will stimulate the plant to branch out and produce more compact growth. You can easily coax any cut-off shoots to begin rooting (see propagation, p. 35).

Preventive measures against pests: Pelargoniums kept indoors may occasionally become infested with white fly or red spider mites (see pests, pp. 26 and 27). A useful preventive measure consists of inserting a pest-control stick into each individual pot. Other pests or diseases are rarely seen on indoor plants.

Preventive measures against fungal disease: Do not position the plants too close together and air them well. Do not wet the leaves when watering. Be sparing with nitrogen-based fertilizers. Use disinfected tools to prune, in order to avoid transferring diseases to other plants

Geraniums in the garden

Watering: As a rule, shrub geraniums in the garden will not need to be watered at all. These plants have a widely spreading root system which can absorb enough moisture from deeper levels of the soil. During long periods of drought and/or in sandy soils, however, the leaves of shrub geraniums may begin to go limp. Now is the time to water.

Regular feeding: If you have mature shrub geraniums, wait until early to mid-spring, when they begin to shoot again, before sprinkling a handful of bio-fertilizer around the plant and raking it lightly into the soil. You need not add inorganic fertilizer, as there are usually enough minerals in regular garden soil. This one food should be enough for the whole summer.

Removing weeds: As soon as weeds start appearing around the shrub geranium, they should be removed so that they will not divert nutrients away from your plants. Small weeds can be pulled out by hand but larger ones with long roots need to be hoed out.

Aerating: Once or twice during the summer, the soil surface around the shrub geraniums should be gently hoed to aerate the soil. This procedure can be carried out in conjunction with the removal of weeds.

Supports and windbreaks: If tall geraniums happen to be positioned in windy places they can easily tip over during the flowering period. Shrub supports, which can be obtained at garden centres etc., will provide good stability and are recommended even for large shrubs.

Infestation by pests is unlikely, as shrub geraniums are very resistant.

Problems, pests and diseases

Important: All plant-protection preparations, even biological ones, must be stored in a place that is inaccessible to children and pets. Only ever spray plants outside – never indoors!

NB: In the gardening trade all plant-protection substances are kept in a locked cabinet and only ever handled by specially trained employees. Seek expert advice about the products you are using and, whenever possible, use biological forms of control.

Pelargoniums on patios and balconies

With proper care and handling, healthy plants should develop sufficient resistance to disease by themselves. While watering, remove any brown, dried-up leaves and old flower stalks in order to prevent decay. Now and again, check the pelargoniums for infestation by pests. Aphids and other pests are often found on the undersides of leaves or on young, soft shoots. The control of aphids (see insect pests) is especially important as they are carriers of the dreaded blight, a bacterial disease (see bacterial diseases).

Indoor pelargoniums

Indoor pelargoniums are very robust. Occasionally they may become infested with red spider mites, aphids or white fly (see pests). If the infestation is severe, you should use an insecticide, following the manufacturer's instructions carefully.

Geraniums in the garden

Just like many other shrubs, geraniums can easily become infested with rust (see fungal diseases) during particularly wet years.

Mistakes in care

Odemas (illustration 1)
Symptoms: Cork-like growths on the undersides of leaves. These occur only on hanging pelargoniums. High humidity favours this condition. Widely varying amounts of water being received by the plant cause its cells to burst and develop into these cork-like masses.

Problems
1. *Odemas*
2. *Waterlogging or salt damage*
3. *Temperatures too low*

Prevention: Water regularly, but not too much. Great differences in the frequency and amount of watering are to be avoided. Try to give the same amount each time, not too much nor too little.
Remedy: Not possible. Odemas do not seem to harm the pelargoniums particularly, being merely unsightly.

Waterlogging or salt damage
(illustration 2)
Symptoms: Wilting, blue green foliage and often brown, rotting root tips.
Prevention: Make sure there are sufficient drainage holes in your plant pots, water sparingly and, if necessary, protect the plants from heavy rain.
Or: reduce feeding.
Remedy: If the plant is not affected too badly, repotting immediately will help. Remove the old soil by shaking it off, trim the root tips gently with scissors and set the pelargonium in new soil.

Temperatures that are too low
(illustration 3)
Symptoms: Yellowish foliage with red leaf edges, especially on older leaves.
Prevention: Do not keep pelargoniums at temperatures of below 4° C (39° F).
Remedy: Raise the temperature and feed more. The discoloration should then disappear.

Pests

Red spider mites (illustration 1)
Symptoms: The leaves turn yellow and fine webs, filled with tiny reddish mites, appear between the leaf veins and the stalks.
Prevention: Regular care (see p. 20) makes the plant more resistant. Avoid dry, warm air in rooms.
Control: Strong insecticides; if the infestation is severe, treatment is often unsatisfactory.

Aphids: (illustration 2)
Symptoms: These pests can be seen quite easily with the naked eye; very often they can be found on the undersides of leaves or on young shoots. The young leaves become twisted; light-coloured

Pests
1 Red spider
  mites
2 Aphids
3 White fly

marks are visible on the leaves.
Prevention: Regular care (see
p. 20) makes the plants more resistant. Avoid dry, warm air in rooms.
Nutrients (fertilizers) should be kept
to a minimum; above all, avoid too
much nitrogen as this will make the
plant cells spongy and unnaturally
large so that they tend to burst
open. Once this has happened,
bacteria may enter.
Control: Biological methods are
very effective; biological sprays
made from a solution of nettles
may help if applied several times.
Otherwise, use commercially available insecticides.

White fly (illustration 3)
Symptoms: The leaves turn yellow
and wither. When the leaves are
touched, tiny white insects fly up.
Regal pelargoniums in particular
tend to become infested.
Prevention: see aphids (p. 26)
Control: Use sticky, coated strips
(bio-friendly greenhouse fly catch-
ers) which lure insects with their
bright colour. Alternatively, try
commonly available insecticides.

Fungal diseases

Pelargonium rust (illustration 1)
Symptoms: The undersides of
leaves are covered with ring-
shaped spore masses which
release a dust when touched. Light
yellow round spots appear on the
uppersides of leaves.
Prevention: Regular aeration, taking care that the leaves do not
become wet (for example, while
watering or in rain).
Control: spray with a fungicide.

Decaying stalks (illustration 2)
Symptoms: The stalks turn black
and then decay, starting at the top
of the roots and moving upwards.
Prevention: Avoid waterlogging.
Temperatures should not drop
below 15° C (59° F).
Control: Spraying with a fungicide.

Grey mould (illustration 3)
Symptoms: Expanses of grey
mould on decaying leaves.
Prevention: Air well and do not set
the plants too close together.
Leaves should not remain wet
overnight; it is better to water

Fungal diseases
1 Pelargonium
  rust
2 Rotting stalks
3 Grey mould

your plants in the mornings.
Control: Spray with a fungicide.

Bacterial diseases

Bacterial blight (Xanthomonas
pelargonii) (also bacterial stem rot)
Symptoms: First phase: small dot-
shaped, light-coloured spots on the
leaves, which quickly become larger and develop into blackish-brown
patches. Healthy leaves turn yellow
and wither fast (illustration 1)

Bacterial
diseases
Bacterial blight
1 First phase
2 Second
  phase
3 Third phase

Second phase: brown bacterial
slime, which appears when the
affected leaf-stalks are bent and
broken (illustration 2). Third phase:
blackish dry rot at the base of the
stalk (illustration 3).
Prevention: When buying plants,
make sure they are healthy. The
bacteria can be transferred by
pests, water or by touch. Tools and
used pots which have come into
contact with infested pelargoniums
should be cleaned and disinfected
before being reused.
Control: None. Destroy affected
plants.

Overwintering

Pelargoniums that have lived on a patio or balcony all summer will need to be overwintered in a different way to those that bloom indoors. The overwintering of shrub geraniums is very different again. Each group has its own individual requirements, which are described below. If you have never tried overwintering your pelargoniums, you will be surprised at how easy it is.

Pelargoniums on patios and balconies

Most people find it difficult to part with pelargoniums that have produced veritable cascades of flowers throughout the summer and into the autumn and, really, there is no reason why they should do so. Overwintering pelargoniums is not a very difficult business provided you have access to the right place. The advantages of this method are that properly overwintered plants will flower even better during the following year (photograph, p. 5) and you will save on the cost of buying new pelargoniums.

My tip: If you are unable to overwinter pelargoniums in the traditional manner because of lack of space, there are space-saving overwintering methods (see p. 30), or you can try cutting the top shoots off your pelargoniums in autumn, before getting rid of them (see propagating, p. 35) and rooting these cuttings as a second generation of plants.

Which plants overwinter best?

● Only overwinter completely healthy, pest-free plants. Before making any other preparations, therefore, you should check that the general health of your pelargoniums is good. Examine the tops and undersides of leaves. The illustrations on pages 26 and 27 will help you to identify pests and diseases. Pelargoniums which show symptoms of bacterial diseases (see p. 27) should be destroyed, so that they cannot infect other plants.
● You can overwinter zonal and hanging pelargoniums but long, trailing plants can take up a lot of space and will need more care when being moved and during storage.
● Pelargoniums in individual pots are especially easy to overwinter, being easier to transport and store than plants in balcony boxes. When they begin to shoot again in the spring, they only need to be moved slightly apart so that they will obtain sufficient space and light for uninterrupted growth. Such overwintering will usually result in beautiful, compact growth.
● Pelargoniums can also be overwintered in a balcony box, often in combination with other plants.
NB: Annual plants (for example,

lobelia or petunias) that are growing in the same box are not suitable for overwintering and will have to be removed. Daisies and fuchsias, on the other hand, can be treated and overwintered in the same way as pelargoniums. In their countries of origin, these shrubby plants are perennials, just as pelargoniums are, but they must be protected from freezing temperatures in European or temperate climates.

Suitable places for overwintering

General rule: The most suitable overwintering areas are bright and frost-free but not too warm. The most suitable of all is a small greenhouse but even light attics, light cellar rooms or garages with access to sufficient daylight make good winter quarters for pelargoniums. Quite unsuitable places are warm cellar rooms, centrally heated rooms or dark rooms.
Pelargoniums that have been overwintered in small greenhouses will start flowering from the middle of spring onwards because they have access to lots of light and are in appropriate cool temperatures. Plants that have overwintered in rooms with less light will produce flowers quite a bit later. However, do not be concerned: after six weeks outside, they will catch up in flowering and you will not be able to tell whether a particular pelargonium was overwintered in a greenhouse or on a windowsill. Give your pelargoniums as much light as possible during the whole period of overwintering and try to keep them close to a window.

My tip: If you have space on only one windowsill for a number of plants, you can buy a collapsible flower shelf made of steel to stand on the windowsill. This gadget has five shelves and can accommodate five filled flowerboxes or many pelargoniums in pots, and will also provide them with plenty of light. It is an excellent device for gardeners who have very little space or who live in flats without a garden.

The rules of overwintering

Preparations
Preparations for overwintering should begin at the end of the summer. Reduce fertilizing from now on. The pelargoniums will gradually become ready for the approaching period of dormancy and will not put out any more new shoots. Examine the plants to see if they are healthy and suitable for overwintering. If everything is all · right, it is time to decide where the best place for overwintering would be. There are many suitable places so almost everyone could manage to overwinter a few plants.

Protection from frosts
Depending on where you live, the first frosts may arrive as early as the beginning of autumn. As pelargoniums cannot tolerate temperatures below freezing, you should find a frost-free place for them – for example, their future overwintering area. Whether you leave the pelargoniums there, or take them outside again into the warm autumn sunlight, is up to you. From early autumn onwards, however, you must keep an eye on the local weather forecasts for frost warnings, so that you will be prepared ahead of time.

Care before dormancy
Once the plants have been settled permanently in their cool, bright winter quarters, they must be tidied up thoroughly. Flowers and dead

Regal pelargoniums were popular in our grandparents' time.

leaves should be snapped off by hand (illustration, p. 23). The overwintering of hanging pelargoniums becomes a little easier if they are cut back a little with scissors. This will not harm the plant at all and will prevent the plant from becoming damaged when it is moved and during the rest period.

Dormancy
With less sunlight and cooler temperatures, the pelargoniums will now sink into a kind of hibernation phase, in which they will remain until the end of winter. Then, as the daylight hours increase noticeably, a new growth phase will begin and the plants will begin to send out new shoots.

Care during dormancy
The optimal overwintering temperature is about 4-10° C (39-50° F). Pelargoniums can tolerate temper-

atures of 2-3° C (36-37° F) for short periods of time but if this goes on too long their leaves will turn reddish (see problems, p. 26). This, however, will return to normal again when the temperature rises. On no account should temperatures sink below 0° C (32° F) as pelargoniums cannot survive freezing.
● Water sparingly during this entire period (approximately once a fortnight). As the pelargoniums will now receive less sunlight than in the summer, they will also need less water. If you water too much, long, weak shoots will form, which are susceptible to disease and break off easily.

Cutting back after overwintering
Use a sharp knife, leaving three or four nodes above the woody brown stalks.

● Stop fertilizing as the plant should now be entering its dormant phase
● Occasionally break off dry leaves and old flower stalks (illustration, p. 23).
● From time to time, check for pests and diseases. If there is any infestation, spray your pelargoniums with commercially available preparations.

Pruning after dormancy
The middle until the end of winter, at the latest, is the period during which you should cut back over-wintered pelargoniums (see illustration). The right place to cut is always the green part of the stalk. Use a sharp knife or scissors and always allow three or four leaf axils to remain on the green stalk. It is from these leaf axils that new shoots will grow after pruning.
Important: Never cut into the woody part of a stalk as these parts of the plant rarely put out new shoots.

Repotting
I recommend planting pelargoniums in new compost after their third overwintering at the latest. When doing this, carefully loosen the plants, together with their complete rootstocks, tip them out of

their overwintering pots and then remove as much soil as possible from the roots without damaging them. After that, plant your pelargoniums in standard potting compost (see planting, p. 12).

New growth
In spring, as the daylight hours increase, temperatures will begin to rise. The pelargoniums will react to this with increased formation of

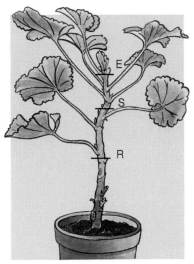

How to cut back
R: cutting back after overwintering; S: pruning; E: pinching out shoot tips

healthy, new shoots and leaves. A little care is now required in order to prepare the pelargoniums for their move outdoors:
● From the last month of winter onwards, water more often.
● Every eight days, add a growth-promoting fertilizer (one with a larger percentage of nitrogen) to your watering can.
● If you have individual pelargoniums in pots make sure they are not

standing too close together. The tips of their leaves should not touch each other. The plants need space in order to grow vigorously.
● The place in which the pelargoniums are kept should be aired often as this will make them more resistant to disease.
● If you pinch out the shoot tips or cut the shoots back a little, you will obtain bushy, compact pelargoniums.
This pinching out can be done by hand using your fingernails to take out the tips of the top shoots (see p. 31). This stimulates growth in the lower buds, which will soon put out more shoots. Cutting back means cutting off some of the particularly long shoots. These can then be used as cuttings (see propagating, p. 35).

My tip: Slow-growing pelargoniums should have their shoot tips pinched out. Fast-growing varieties, such as the hanging cascade pelargoniums, will respond to cutting back by ceasing to produce only a few long, trailing shoots and, instead, will branch out and grow more compactly.
At the end of dormancy: After the last cold snap in spring, put your pelargoniums outside.

Space-saving overwintering methods
The following are two fairly uncommon methods employed by some hobby gardeners. Be warned that not every pelargonium will survive this!

Overwintering in a plastic bag
● Water the pelargoniums well.
● Cut each plant back to about 15 cm (6 in).
● Carefully remove the plant, together with its rootstock and the surrounding soil, and put it in a plas-

tic bag. Freezer bags are especially suitable as they are quite tough.

● Tie the plastic bag up tightly so that no moisture can escape. This will prevent the pelargoniums from drying out.

● Use empty flowerboxes (a box 1 m or 20 in long will accommodate about seven to ten plants) to store the plants, or suspend them from a "washing line" stretched across or near a window.

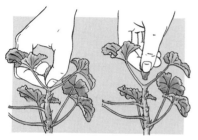

Pinching out shoot tips
Pinch out the uppermost shoot tips with your fingernails.

● Check the moisture occasionally and add water if necessary.
● From the first month of spring onwards, begin planting the pelargoniums in pots again.
● Overwintering temperatures should be 6-10 C (43-50 F). The plants will need lots of light!

Overwintering in paper
● Remove dead flowers and leaves and take the pelargoniums out of their containers.
● Leaves and stalks should be dry and the soil around the roots should be only slightly moist.
● Lightly shake some of the soil off the roots. Do not remove all of it!
● Wrap each pelargonium individually (roots, leaves and flowers) in newspaper.
● Place these packages in a box and let them overwinter in a frost-free place in the cellar.

● At the beginning of the last month of winter, take these packages out of their winter quarters and cut back the shoots (see p. 30).
● Plant the pelargoniums in fresh standard potting compost and stand them in a warm room.
● As soon as new shoots become visible, give them as much light as possible!

Indoor pelargoniums
Overwintering in a warm room

In their subtropical countries of origin, pelargoniums do not have a period of dormancy and they will continue to flower all year round. This is why they may produce an odd flower even in winter if placed in the window of a warm room. If pelargoniums are kept in a warm room all winter, they must be fed and watered regularly (see p. 23).

Overwintering methods for obtaining lots of flowers

Fancy-leaved pelargoniums
These should be overwintered like pelargoniums on patios and balconies (see p. 28).

Scented-leaved and wild pelargoniums
Keep them near a window in a warm room until the end of winter, then stand them in a bright, cool room at an optimal temperature of 5° C (41° F). Keep them cool in this fashion for about four to six weeks but do not water or feed them during this time. It will be sufficient just to spray the leaves with water quite frequently. During this cool period, flower-buds will form .
● After four to six weeks, put the

pelargoniums in a warm room again, in front of a window, but still do not water them. Carry on spraying them instead.
● From early spring onwards, begin to water them carefully and feed them very sparingly, putting only half of the recommended dose of liquid fertilizer in the water.
● From the last month of spring onwards, continue with normal care (see p. 23).

Regal pelargoniums
These plants will need a cool period of four to six weeks, just like the scented-leaved and wild pelargoniums. During this time, they should be watered very sparingly. From early spring onwards, water more and give a normal weekly dose of liquid fertilizer in water.

Geraniums in the garden

Every year in the autumn, the parts above ground will die down and the plant will produce new shoots again in the spring.
In late autumn, cut off the leaves and shoots that look brown approximately 20 cm (8 in) above the ground. Make sure you do not cut the above ground parts right down to the soil, enabling moisture from the soil to seep into the heart of the roots via the exposed cut surfaces, which would encourage decay. This rule applies to all garden shrubs. The robust geranium will not need any more care than this. Winter protection will not be needed. From early to mid-spring, the shrub will start shooting again. When the new shoots have reached a height of 5-10 cm (2-4 in), sprinkle a handful of bio-fertilizer around the plant, then work the fertilizer into the soil, so that it will dissolve better.

Propagating made easy

Generally speaking, very few gardeners use seed for propagating geraniums and pelargoniums. Which plants are most suited to this method and how to do it are both explained in this chapter. Propagating by means of cuttings is even easier and, like overwintering, makes it unnecessary for you to buy new plants the following year. It is also interesting and most enjoyable to propagate successfully.

Pelargoniums on patios and balconies

The right time to propagate

Pelargoniums can be propagated by using cuttings (vegetative) or from seeds (generative).
Propagating from cuttings is possible with all pelargoniums, but propagating from seed is only done with certain F_1 hybrids (see My tip, p. 8), wild pelargoniums and shrub geraniums. Both methods of propagating are possible all year round.
If you wish to have pelargoniums that are carrying lots of buds by the end of the last cold snap in spring, you should follow the propagation schedules given below:
Propagating from seed: Sow the seeds from the middle of the first month of winter until the end of the second month at the very latest (method, see below).
Propagating from cuttings: Take shoots for cuttings at any time from late summer to the middle of the first month of spring at the very latest and plant them at once (method, p. 35).

Propagating from seed

There are two methods of sowing seeds, in peat pellets or in seed trays, and each method requires different care. The germination and growth of young plants is equally successful using either method.

Method 1 – sowing seeds in peat pellets
You will need:
● a mini-propgator for use indoors, with a transparent cover (obtainable in the gardening trade at reasonable prices), or a plastic tray with a light-permeable plastic hood or glass plate;
● peat pellets (sold in garden centres);
● pelargonium seed;
● seeding compost (germ-free, special compost for seeds and cuttings, from garden centres etc.);
● plastic or clay pots with a diameter of 11 cm (4¼ in);
● standard potting compost.

Procedure
● Place the dry, wheel-shaped peat pellets in the plastic tray of your mini-propagator and carefully pour lukewarm water over them (p. 34).
● These peat discs will quickly swell to several times their previous size. Add more lukewarm water until no more is soaked up. Pour away any surplus water.
● Put one seed in each peat pellet and push it in with your finger to a depth of about 1 cm (⅛ in), so that the soil envelopes it.
● Stand the plastic tray of seeds in a bright, warm position; the optimal place might be on a windowsill above a radiator.
● Place the plastic cover (or plate of glass) over the seed tray. Covering the seeds should promote the right kind of moist/warm atmosphere in the propagator. The seeds need a germination temperature of 18-20° C (64-68° F).

Development and care
A few days after planting the seeds, you will see the first delicate leaflets peeping out of the soil.
During the first fourteen days after sowing, the tiny plants will need a lot of care and attention as they are very delicate and can be damaged quite easily.
● If condensation develops on the inside of the plastic cover, you will have to lift it off to air it in order to avoid the growth of mould. Many such mini-propagators have ventilation slits that can be opened and shut. If your propagator does not have these, simply place a small stick between the plastic tray and the cover (see p. 34). Whenever necessary, ventilate the propagator in this way for one or two hours each day.
● If the sunlight is very intense, it is a good idea to place some newspaper over the plastic cover in

Semi-pendent pelargonium "Schöne von Grenchen" will produce glowing red flowers even in semi-shade.

order to protect the pelargonium seedlings from burns.

● Use your fingers to check whether the peat pellets are still moist. You will probably have to add a little lukewarm water from time to time.

Three weeks after sowing the pelargoniums will be several centimetres high. Toughen up the young plants by removing the cover.

During the following weeks the pelargoniums will grow very quickly. When the leaves of the young plants begin to touch each other, they should be moved apart so that the plants can carry on growing without being restricted.

Five weeks after sowing the temperature should be lowered to 16° C (61° F) (the best thing to do is to place the pelargoniums in a bright, cool room) so that the plants can toughen up.

About ten weeks after sowing you will see little white rootlets growing out of the peat pellets. Now plant the young pelargoniums in a large plastic or clay pot with a diameter of 11 cm (4¼ in). This is the pot that the young plant will remain in until it is finally taken outside to be planted on a balcony or patio. When you plant the pelargonium in its final pot, it should be left in the old soil but you should add a little extra standard potting compost. Make sure the plant does not sit any deeper in the soil than it was before.

Sowing seeds

Pour lukewarm water on to the peat pellets and allow them to swell up. Using a folded sheet of paper, place one seed on each peat pellet, press it in to about 1 cm (⅓ in) deep and cover it with soil.
After germination, the cover should be removed for ventilation if condensation develops.

Method 2 – sowing seed in special seeding compost

You will need:
● a mini-propagator for use indoors, with a transparent cover, or a plastic tray with a light-permeable plastic cover or glass plate (p. 32);
● seeding compost;
● pelargonium seed (obtainable in garden centres etc.);
● a dibber;
● peat propagation pots with a diameter of 6 cm (2 in). (Made of pressed peat, these round or square pots, in various different sizes, are obtainable at garden centres etc. The advantage of them is that the plants need not be removed from the pot as their roots will grow through the pot wall);
● plastic or clay pots with a diameter of 11 cm (4¼ in);
● standard potting compost.

Procedure

● Pour special seeding compost into the plastic tray, almost up to the edge. If necessary, crumble it a little to distribute it evenly.
● Carefully fill the tray with lukewarm water until the soil is well moistened.
● Sow the seeds in plots of 2.5 x 2.5 cm (1 x 1 in), using a folded piece of paper as an aid (see illustration). Lightly press the seeds into the soil with your finger (about 1 cm or ⅓ in deep) and cover them with soil.
● Place the plastic tray in a bright, warm position, the best place would be a windowsill above a radiator.
● Now place the plastic cover (or plate of glass) over the seeding tray as the seeds will need moist, warm air to germinate at a temperature of 18-20° C (64-68° F).

Development and care

During the first three weeks after sowing the same care should be given as described for sowing in peat pellets (see p. 32).
When the little plants are big enough for their leaves to touch those of their neighbours, they must be pricked out so that they have more space in which to grow.
● Pricking out is quite simple: lift the tiny pelargoniums out of the soil carefully using a dibber (illustration right).
● If the roots are especially long, they can be pinched off with your fingernails (illustration right), which makes replanting easier.
● Now put a little seeding compost in small peat pots (6 cm or 2⅓ in), very carefully insert the young plants and add as much soil

as necessary to fill up the pot.
● The seedlings should be planted right up to their leaves as more tiny roots will form above the existing roots.
● After all the seedlings have been pricked out, clean the plastic tray, which can now serve as a base for all the little pots.
● Stand the plantlets in the plastic tray and water them gently.
As growth increases, the pelargoniums should be moved apart so that the tips of the leaves do not touch.
Five weeks after sowing the temperature should be reduced to 16° C (61° F) (the best plan is to stand the pelargoniums in a bright, cool room), so that the plants can toughen up.

Pricking out
Loosen the seedling in the soil using the thin end of the dibber. Shorten the root tip.

Planting the seedling
Make a hole with the thick end of the dibber. Insert the seedling up to its leaves and press down lightly.

About ten weeks after sowing, the roots will have developed to the point where the plant will now require a larger pot. Do not remove the small peat pot but simply plant the young pelargonium, together with its pot and a little standard potting compost, in a plastic clay pot with a diameter of 11 cm (4¼ in). Make sure that the plants do not sit any deeper in the soil than they were before.

My tip: If done with care, both methods of sowing seed should result in the same time being taken for the plants to develop. You will find, however, that using peat pellets is less time-consuming as the seedlings do not need to be pricked out.

Propagating from cuttings

If you already grow pelargoniums, you will have the opportunity of taking cuttings from the mother plants for growing into new plants.

The best pelargonium cutting
● will be 7-10 cm (just under 3-4 in) long;
● will have at least one set of fully developed leaves;
● will have a stalk that is crisp, fresh and deep green. Do not take light green, young, soft shoots (they tend to decay when planted) nor older, brown, woody shoots as they will not root easily.

Propagating equipment
● a disinfected knife (so that no germs are transferred while taking the cutting);
● peat pellets (obtainable in garden centres etc.) or peat propagating pots with a diameter of 6 cm (2⅓ in) (made of pressed peat, round or square, in various sizes and obtainable at garden centres

etc.), the advantage being that the plants need not be removed from the pots as their roots will grow right through the wall;
● mini-propagator for use indoors, with a cover (available at reasonable prices in garden centres etc.) or a plastic tray with a light-permeable plastic cover or glass plate;
● seeding compost (germ-free special compost for seeds and cuttings, made of peat, loam and essential nutrients, obtainable in garden centres etc.);
● plastic or clay pots with a diameter of 11 cm (4¼ in);
● standard potting compost (obtainable in garden centres etc.).

Method
● A few hours before taking the cuttings, water the mother plants so that the cuttings are not limp, but strong and crisp.
● Look for suitable cuttings on the mother plant (description left) and, using a disinfected knife, cut them off approximately 2 cm (1 in) below a set of leaves (illustration right). The cuttings should have stalks of about 2 cm (1 in), so that they can be planted deep enough.
● Buds or flowers on cuttings should be removed (illustration, p. 23), so that all the energy will go into the growth of the new plant.
● Plant the cuttings immediately after taking them from the mother plant – either in well soaked peat pellets or in small peat propagating pots filled with seeding compost.
● Plant the cuttings at a depth of about 2 cm (1 in) in the soil, press down gently and water so that the soil envelopes the unrooted cutting.
● Place the plantlets, in their peat pellets or peat propagating pots, in a plastic tray and cover this. The cuttings will thus live in an extremely humid environment and evaporation through their leaves will be

reduced to a minimum. As the shoots are still rootless at this point, and water absorption from below is not yet possible, it is vital to cover the plants during the first week.

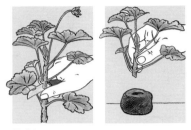

Taking a cutting
Cut between two leaf axils with a sharp, disinfected knife. Break off the bud and stalk with your fingernails where the stalk grows from the main stem. Insert the cutting into a peat pellet and press down gently.

● Keep the cuttings in a very bright place (a window is best) at a room temperature of 18-20° C (64-68° F).

Development and care
A few days after planting, a callus (new plant tissue) will form on the cutting and, soon afterwards, the first little roots will appear.

● If condensation appears inside the cover, you will have to air it (p. 32) or there is a risk of grey mould growing on the cuttings or on the soil.

● If the sunlight is extremely bright, lay a sheet of newspaper over the plastic cover, to protect the plants from burns.

● *After two weeks* you can remove the cover as the roots will have formed by now and will be supplying the plants with water from below.

Four weeks after planting you can expect to see many young roots growing out of the peat pots – a sign that your propagating efforts have been successful.

After a further three to five weeks, plant the growing cuttings in plastic or clay pots with a diameter of 11 cm (4¼ in), adding a little standard potting compost. The pelargoniums should be left in their old soil. Propagating pots which are infiltrated with roots should never be removed as the rootstock would be destroyed in the process and the plant would receive an irreversible shock, affecting its growth. Make sure that the plants do not sit any deeper in the soil than they were before. The pelargoniums should remain in these peat pots until they are moved outside, on to a patio or balcony, for planting.

Care of the young plants

No matter which method of propagating you have chosen, planting the pelargonium in its final pot marks the transition from the infant stage to the youthful stage of the plant. From now on, care is the same for the former seedling as it is for the former cutting.

Place in a bright, cool position: At this point the pelargoniums should be kept in a place that is as light as possible (for example, a sunny windowsill or, ideally, a small greenhouse) and relatively cool (16° C/61° F).

Pinching out shoots: Two to four weeks after planting in their final pots, the pelargonium plants will have grown considerably. Now is the time to pinch out shoots (see p. 31), which means removing the top shoot tips with your fingernails. This should be done by the middle of the first month of spring. If you pinch the shoot tips out too late, flowering will be delayed.

Toughening up: By the end of the second month of spring your home-propagated pelargoniums will have developed fat buds. It is time to toughen them up now so that they can continue growing outside without suffering a temperature shock, which would affect their development. Ventilate the room frequently and keep it as cool as possible.

Check for pests: Check your plants occasionally for pests (see p. 26). Aphids should be controlled with the usual commercial products, as they may carry bacterial blight (see diseases, p. 27).

Avoid heat and cramped conditions: Zonal and hanging pelargoniums should not receive too much heat during the second and last months of spring and should not be placed too close together, or else their shoots may easily become long and weak.

Cultivating pelargoniums quickly

This method uses cuttings that are taken during the first two weeks of spring. You may utilize the cuttings that are created when you cut back the plant after dormancy (overwintering, p. 30).

● Use a plastic or clay pot with a diameter of 11 cm (4¼ in) and seeding compost.

● Plant three to four cuttings around the outer edge of the pot.

● After watering gently, draw a transparent polythene sheet over the pot and cuttings, so that no moisture can evaporate but the cuttings are not impeded in their growth.

● Stand the pelargoniums in a very bright place and encourage them to root at temperatures of 18-20° C (64-68° F).

● After two weeks, the polythene may be removed, as the cuttings will now have roots.

● Let the plants grow without pinching out shoot tips.

● During this phase, do not allow the surrounding temperatures to drop below 16° C (61° F).

● By the end of the spring you will have a splendid harvest of robust pelargoniums which should be on the point of flowering.

Indoor pelargoniums

Fancy-leaved pelargoniums

These pelargoniums can only be propagated from cuttings. The method to follow for propagating and aftercare of the fully grown plant should be the same as for pelargoniums kept outside (see p. 35). As fancy-leaved pelargoniums do not need to bloom at a certain time, they can be propagated at any time during the year. Propagating from seeds is not possible.

Regal pelargoniums

Regal pelargoniums can also only be propagated from cuttings. Furthermore, cuttings from these species do not always produce

Pelargoniums are a popular decorative plant for hotels and inns. Hanging varieties on an old wooden bridge.

roots readily either. It is best to dip the cut surface and stalk of the cuttings 2 cm (1 in) deep in rooting powder (obtainable in garden centres etc.). This will help them to form a callus (see p. 35).

If possible, take and grow cuttings from regal pelargoniums during the summer, as experience has shown they are less likely to root well during the winter season.

The method of propagating and aftercare is the same as for pelargoniums that grow outside (see p. 36).

Scented-leaved and wild pelargoniums

Propagating from seed

Wild pelargoniums can be propagated from seed. You will not, however, be able to obtain these in the ordinary gardening trade and may have to try private growers instead. Contact can be established via small ads placed in plant magazines etc. For the method of sowing see page 32.

Propagating from shoot tips

Scented-leaved and wild pelargoniums are usually propagated from cuttings as this is a fast and easy way to obtain robust, healthy plants.

The right time to take cuttings: Cuttings should be taken from the parent plant between the end of spring and late autumn. Experience has shown that the best results are obtained during the summer months when there is maximum light and heat.

Suitable varieties: Note that not all scented-leaved and wild pelargoniums are equally easy to propagate.

Easily rooted species and varieties are: *Pelargonium tomentosum, Pelargonium capitatum, Pelargonium fragrans, Pelargonium papilonaceum* and "Princess Anne".

Reluctant rooting species and varieties are: *Pelargonium gibbosum, Pelargonium cunanifolium*, and "Countess of Scarborough".

Propagating soil: For propagating, use compost that you have mixed yourself, consisting of one third seeding compost, one third sand and one third Perlite, which is finely ground volcanic rock (obtainable at garden centres etc.). This mixture will be highly water-permeable.

Plant containers: Plant the cuttings in previously well-soaked (p. 17) clay pots with a diameter of 6 cm (2⅓ in).

Important: Do not use peat for scented-leaved and wild pelargoniums, so that as little water as possible is retained around the sensitive roots. For this reason, the cuttings should not be planted in peat pellets nor in peat propagating pots.

Position: The cuttings should be watered sparingly and left to form roots at a minumum temperature of 18-20° C (64-68° F) on a sunny windowsill.

Development: The time it takes for scented-leaved and wild pelargoniums to develop will vary according to species. Watch the cuttings carefully. When they have grown, remove one from its pot (illustration p. 18) and check to see how far the roots have developed.

Planting in the final pot: If the roots have reached the edge of the propagating pot, it is time to transfer the young plants to their final pots, which should be clay pots with a diameter of 11 cm (4¼ in). The lower third of each pot should be filled with Hortag or large pieces of broken pot and then filled with the compost mixture described above. This drainage layer will help surplus water to drain away.

Further care: Keep the young plants in a sunny, warm place. Take care that the roots are never left standing in water, as they will rot very easily. For scented-leaved and wild pelargoniums, a cool, dry period of four to six weeks will be required at the beginning of the second month of winter: the temperature should be 5° C (41° F), and the plants should not be watered, although you may spray them lightly. After this period, raise the temperature very gradually and give a little more water. These procedures will ensure a rich harvest of flowers.

Geraniums in the garden

Propagating from seed

Sow shrub geranium seed in seeding trays in the middle and third months of spring.

As the seeds of geraniums are much smaller than those of pelargoniums, it is not a good idea to plant them in peat pellets as it would be very difficult to place individual seeds in such beds.

The seed trays should be kept in a bright, warm place (18-20° C/64-68° F).

As soon as the seed has germinated and the plantlets are large enough, they should be pricked out (see p. 34) and planted in small peat propagating pots.

As soon as roots appear through the walls of the pots, the pots should be planted outside in flowerbeds.

Propagating by division

You may divide an older plant in the spring, while the shoots are still small. For this purpose dig the plant up and divide it, with a knife or spade, into several parts, which are then planted separately. This method is suitable for many garden shrubs.

The zonal pelargonium "Bern" will flourish all summer long, even in a flowerbed.

Baskets, pedestals, standards and combinations with other plants

Imagine the effect of two pelargoniums, trained into the shape of pillars, standing on either side of a patio door or a pergola decorated with hanging baskets of pelargoniums. The possibilities for using these versatile plants for decoration are endless.

Pelargoniums on patios and balconies

Pelargoniums are very versatile plants – they will even grow downwards – and they get along well with other plants. These features make possible a wide range of ornamental uses. Hanging baskets can be planted with hanging pelargoniums. Vigorously growing varieties can be trained into standards or grown on pedestals within a relatively short time, and pelargoniums can also be incorporated into the most magnificent colour combinations when planted together with other colourful summer flowers.

Pelargoniums in hanging baskets

Around your house there may be protruding eaves, a roofed-over area or a pergola (see p. 19) where you can put up hanging baskets. When choosing such sites, however, do not forget that hanging baskets must be within easy reach for watering and general care.

Suitable plants

Use hanging pelargoniums for planting in baskets, perferably plants of the "cascade" varieties (see p. 44), which come in shades of wine red, brick red, lilac and pink. They are especially suitable for baskets, for three reasons:

● They can cope in unfavourable positions, such as shady or draughty corners.
● They are "self-tidying", which means that the small petals roll up as they wither so that they are scarcely visible any longer. This is a definite advantage for baskets that hang high up and/or are difficult to reach.
● They flower very abundantly. The hanging varieties known as mini-cascades are unrivalled in quantities of flowers produced.

My tip: If you have a basket that you want to fill with plants, when you buy your hanging pelargoniums, check to what length they are likely to grow. Mini-cascades will grow to 50 cm (20 in) at the most. Other cascade varieties can grow to a length of 1.5 m (5 ft).

Combinations with other flowering plants

If you do not wish to confine yourself to shades of red only for your hanging baskets, you may create symphonies of colour by using other plants too. Hanging varieties of blue lobelia are popular basket plants, as are calceolaria – yellow; marguerite daisies – white and yellow; hanging verbena – pink; and brachycomes – sky blue.

Method

Plant containers: Plastic baskets with a removable dish underneath (obtainable at garden centres etc. in all sizes) are very practical. They do not weigh much when empty and are easy to clean. Remember that the baskets will increase in weight as the plants grow and will need a device for hanging them up that can cope with the strain.

Planting: Plant no more than three hanging pelargoniums in a basket with a diameter of 25 cm (10 in) (for soil and planting methods, see pp. 12 and 18). Make sure a watering space of at least 2 cm (1 in) is left at the top when planting, so that soil is not washed out every time you water the plants.

Tips on care

Care for pelargoniums in hanging baskets in the same way as for those in pots or flowerboxes (see care, p. 20).

Watering: Mini-cascades tend to react rather sensitively to overwatering and cool temperatures during the first few weeks and will be inclined to develop root rot rather quickly. For this reason, make sure that no waterlogging occurs in the dish underneath, or even remove the dish if the position allows this. Sometimes pelargoniums in baskets are neglected when it comes to watering, because of their elevated position.

Pelargoniums in hanging baskets (here the cultivar "Galilee") should be fed frequently!

Do not forget them and remember that, even in heavy rain, basket plants will receive hardly any water if they are sheltered or under cover.
Feeding: Basket pelargoniums need feeding (see p. 22). The cascade varieties, in particular, should receive regular weekly doses of compound fertilizer in their water.
Cutting back: If the pelargoniums grow too long, you may cut them back at any time (see p. 30), using a sharp knife to cut to the desired length.

Overwintering
The overwintering of pelargoniums in baskets is the same as for pelargoniums in pots or boxes (see p. 28).

Standards

Training a standard is not as difficult as many people think and will take exactly a year. If you begin the growing of rooted cuttings in the spring (see p. 35), with consistent care you should be able to brighten up your balcony or patio with a fully grown standard by the following year. The best way is to start with several cuttings, of which only one, the strongest, will end up being trained further as a standard.

Suitable pelargoniums
Zonal pelargoniums and hanging pelargoniums can be trained as standards. Zonal hybrids are easier to train.

Decorative underplanting
Low-growing annuals, such as alyssum, brachycomes or *Sanvitalia procumbens*, are very suitable for planting under standards. They bloom all summer long but will have to be renewed every year.

How to train standards
Start in early spring with a few robust cuttings that you have taken from overwintered plants and have rooted (see p. 35), or buy ready-rooted cuttings in a garden centre.
Planting: As soon as the cuttings have rooted well, each individual cutting should be planted in a plastic or clay pot with a diameter of 11 cm (4 in) (see p. 36).
Soil: Standard potting compost or a commercial potting compost which you should mix with basic fertilizer (p. 15).
Regular feeding: Three weeks after planting, it will be time to give your plants some liquid compound fertilizer (p. 22) in water.
Encouraging upward growth: As the plant grows, the main stem will form side shoots and buds which you should pinch off immediately with your fingers (illustration, p. 23) so that all the growing energy goes into the height of the plant.
Final choices: During this growth phase, you will be able to decide which plant is especially suited to further cultivation. Plants should be chosen as standards if their main stem is especially straight, strong and tall. Pelargoniums with crooked main stems are unsuitable, as are pelargoniums which obviously lag behind the others in their growth.
Repotting: In late spring the main stem should be about 50 cm (20 in) tall. Plant the pelargonium in a clay pot with a diameter of 18 cm (7 in).
Soil: standard potting compost or fertilized potting compost.
Tying to a support: After repotting, drive a 1.2 m (4 ft) long stick in beside the stem as a support for the plant and loosely tie the stem

to it with raffia or twine. The tie is intended to give the stem support without constricting it.

Further care: Three weeks after repotting, start putting liquid compound fertilizer into the water once a week and continue to pinch out laterals and flowerbuds.

At a height of 75 cm (30 in): Carry on pinching out laterals and flowerbuds until the stem has reached this height (measured from the edge of the pot) but leave laterals and leaves above that height as they will form the head later on. The flowerbuds, however, should still be removed.

At a height of 1 m (40 in): At the end of the first month of summer and the beginning of the second month, the pelargonium should have attained a height of about 1 m (40 in). Now cut off the top of the main stem. Of the laterals that have grown out to over 75 cm (30 in), leave the topmost five or six as they will form branches for the future head. If possible, these laterals should be distributed evenly around the stem.

A tall, elegant standard
This speciman measures 2.53 m (8 ft 5 in). It was developed over a period of two years from four cuttings of a cascade variety.

Repotting: When the laterals have grown a little larger (about 5 cm or 2 in), transfer the standard into its final pot, preferably a heavy clay pot, as this will give the pelargonium the required stability.

Soil: standard potting compost or a fertilized commercial potting compost.

This repotting procedure will probably require two people:
● Place the standard next to the new clay pot.
● Fill the new pot with soil up to about a level of 5 cm (2 in).
● At this point, you will need a helper to support the standard plant during the whole operation of repotting, so that it does not break.
● In order to extract the standard from its old pot unharmed, it will have to be laid on the ground. To do this, tip the pot slowly, without tearing off any roots or sections of roots. The support stick should be left in its position in the soil.
● Lift the standard upright by encircling the rootstock with both hands and then place it in the new pot.
● With your helper still supporting the standard, fill the pot with extra soil all around the rootstock. The soil should be pressed down firmly so that the plant stands up straight, but not so hard that it seems as if it had been cemented in!

Pinching tips out of laterals: once the laterals have grown to a length of about 25 cm (10 in), pinch out their shoot tips (p. 31), so that they will branch out again. Soon a compact head will form with some first flowers which should no longer be pinched out.

Care during the first year
The standard has now reached its final shape. The following procedures should be carried out until overwintering begins:
Feeding: Put liquid compound fertilizer in the water once a week until the end of the summer. During the first month of autumn feed only once every fortnight, then stop watering altogether so that the plant can enter its dormant phase.
Tidying: Continue to remove leaves and flowerbuds which form on the stem.
Support stick: Occasionally check the places where the stem has been tied to the support stick to make sure there is no constriction.

Overwintering
Before the first frosts appear, take the standard inside and place it in a bright, cool room. It should be overwintered like all other pelargoniums that have been outside (see p. 28).
When the pelargonium standard starts putting out shoots the following spring, you should pinch out the tips once more, by the second month of spring at the latest (see p. 31), in order to obtain a compact head. From the middle of the last month of spring onwards, the pelargonium will bloom in full splendour. If you leave pinching out the shoot tips until later, you will delay flowering.

Tips on care during the second year
General care: Pelargonium standards should be cared for all year round just like all other pelargoniums on patios and balconies (p. 20).
Cutting back: Long, protruding shoots which grow out of the head shape, should be cut off (see p. 30).
Support stick: During the second year, replace the support stick. The new one should be thicker (with a diameter of 2 cm/just under 1 in) and reach right into the centre of the standard head, so that the plant is given plenty of support as it grows.

Pedestals
Pelargoniums grown on pedestals will enhance the appearance of any patio, balcony or bare corner.

Suitable plants
Both hanging and zonal pelargoniums are suitable for this purpose. Hanging plants are more suitable, however, as they generally grow much more vigorously.

Method
● In early spring, plant three rooted pelargonium cuttings in a clay pot with a diameter of at least 25 cm (10 in). The best pots are square, terracotta ones, as they offer great stability.
Soil: standard potting compost or simple commercial compost mixed with basic fertilizer (see p. 15).
● Drive a long stick into the middle of the pot of pelargoniums. All growing shoots should be tied loosely to this, using raffia or twine.
● Do not remove the laterals, but continue to cut them back until the second month of spring, so that, very gradually, they will grow into a compact cone shape.
● From the middle of the second month of spring onward, allow the shoots to grow and buds will soon begin to form.

Care
Pelargoniums grown on pedestals should be looked after exactly like pelargoniums in flowerboxes or pots (see p. 20).

Combinations of pelargoniums and other summer annuals
Make a point of checking the arrangement for:
● colours that will blend in well to suit the surroundings in

which the arrangement is set;
● colours of flowers that go together;
● large and small flowers to balance the arrangement;
● different kinds of leaves (colour, shape and size) which may enhance the general effect;
● plants that go together with respect to their growth and shape (for flowerboxes, for example, it is preferable to plant hanging plants at the front and upright plants at the back).

Suitable plants

Choose sun-loving annuals that will bloom all summer long and will not grow too tall for a balcony box arrangement. They come in many beautiful shades, with large flowers (petunias, for example), delicate flowers (lobelia), hanging flowers (hanging verbena) or very upright flowers.

Tips on care

Mixed plantings containing pelargoniums should be cared for in the same way as pelargoniums in flowerboxes or pots (see p. 20).
Cutting back accompanying plants: In wet years some summer flowers may outstrip the pelargoniums in their growth. Petunias and large daisies can become so large and overpowering that some cutting back will be called for. Petunias can stand rigorous pruning. With marguerite daisies, however, do not cut back to the woody parts!

Overwintering

Before overwintering begins, remove the summer annuals from the flowerbox as they will not survive the winter. Take this opportunity to move the pelargoniums to individual pots which, in turn, will stimulate more compact growth the following year (see p. 28).

A combination of various hanging pelargoniums growing on a pedestal.

Indoor pelargoniums

Pelargoniums kept indoors – the regal, fancy-leaved and scented-leaved varieties – will not offer the same wide range of uses as the zonal or hanging hybrids on balconies and patios. Some varieties, however, can be trained into standards.

Suitable plants

Regal pelargoniums are quite suitable for training into standards. Among the scented-leaved and wild pelargoniums, to date only a few varieties are known to be suitable, these being the large-flowering pelargonium (*Pelargonium grandiflorum*), the cultivar "Princess Anne" and all scented-leaved hybrids (see p. 50).

Method

Indoor pelargoniums should be trained as standards in exactly the same way as zonal or hanging hybrids (see p. 40). However, you must also take into consideration the care requirements of the various species (see pp. 23, 50).

Geraniums in the garden

Shrub geraniums cannot be trained into special shapes. They do, however, blend well into arrangements of plants incorporating other shrubs. They come in colours that range through blue, white and violet, as well as many shades of pink and red. They are grown as tall shrubs and also in the form of cushions (see pp. 58, 59).

Pelargoniums for patios and balconies

In this section you will be introduced to some popular varieties of zonal (see pp. 46, 47), hanging and semi-pendent (see pp. 48, 49) pelargoniums. An indication of their appearance, characteristics and care should help you when choosing plants.

Zonal pelargoniums

Zonal pelargoniums are hybrids (bastard crosses) whose parents were *Pelargonium zonale* (*zonale* = girdle) and *Pelargonium inquinans* (see illustrations, p.8). To date, hundreds of different varieties have been bred. Depending on which parent is more dominant in a particular variety, a brownish "girdle" or ring marking can be seen on each leaf.

Appearance and similarities
All zonal pelargonium hybrids grow upright. Nearly all varieties have relatively large leaves and robust, slightly hairy shoots. The flowers grow on long stalks and consist of umbels with varying numbers of individual blooms. Some zonal pelargonium flowers are single but most are double.
Note: Single flowers means that the individual flower has five petals like its parents. Double flowers have more petals, as, through breeding, they have developed extra petals which have metamorphosed from the stamens and style. Zonal pelargoniums come in many colours: shades of glowing red, pink and bright pink. Shades of salmon pink and pure white are fairly rare but can be used for unusual combinations of plants.

Zonal pelargoniums are especially suitable as:
● they can be arranged in combinations with other summer flowers;
● they can be trained into standards without a great deal of trouble (see p. 40);
● overwintering presents no great problems (p. 28);
● they can be propagated easily from cuttings taken from shoot tips (see p. 35).

Hanging and semi-pendent pelargoniums

The hanging pelargoniums (*Pelargonium – Peltatum* hybrids) were created by crossing the wild *Pelargonium peltatum* (*pelta* = shield) with other wild species. The name refers to the leaves, which, in contrast with the softer, hairy leaves of zonal pelargoniums, are fleshy, thick and shield-shaped. The semi-pendent pelargoniums (*Pelargonium – Zonale* x *Peltatum* hybrids) are hybrids which were produced by crossing zonal and hanging pelargoniums. They are also known as semi-hanging or semi-peltates.

Appearance and similarities
In their South African homeland, hanging or semi-pendent pelargoniums may grow shoots up to 2 m (40 in) long. These shoots trail on the ground or climb, creeper-like, into higher bushes. The flowers of bred varieties are partly single, partly double. They come in glorious shades of red, pink, deep pink and even white.

Cascade varieties
The cascade varieties are a special group, within the hanging pelargoniums, which was rediscovered a few years ago in France. Their outer appearance distinguishes them quite clearly from other hanging pelargoniums, as their flowers look very similar to those of wild pelargoniums (see photo on inside front cover) with single, delicately shaped petals and small flowers. Their vigorous growth and abundance of flowers, however, is unrivalled among all other pelargoniums. Well-cared-for cascade varieties (for example, "Ville de Paris", see p. 49, No. 4, "Lachscascade" or "Feuercascade", see p. 49 No. 3) can form trailing shoots of up to 1.5 m (5 ft) in length, which are completely covered in flowers, while the mini-cascades (for example, "Lila Mini-Cascade" and "Rote Mini-Cascade") can grow up to 50 cm (20 in). Another advantage is that the cascade varieties are "self-tidying". When the flowers die, their petals wither and curl up so small that you can hardly see them. They do not fall. Anyone who has spent the summer sweeping up fallen red or pink petals under a large balcony, will appreciate what a boon this can be.

My tip: Overwintering the very long cascade varieties can be a little tedious. Instead, why not take cuttings in the autumn and overwinter the young plants.

Pelargoniums for patios and balconies

Hanging and semi-pendent pelargoniums are especially suitable:

● as popular, easy-to-care-for plants for hanging baskets and flowerboxes;

● in plant arrangements with upright summer-flowering plants, where they provide the ideal downward-growing element.

Tips on care

In brief, the following are the main requirements of pelargoniums on patios and balconies:

● a lot of sun (see p. 12);
● nutrient-rich soil (see p. 12);
● lots of nutrients (see pp. 15 and 22);
● water, though not too much (see p. 20);

● no waterlogging (see plant containers, p. 16);
● no frost (see overwintering p. 29).

My tip: The cascade varieties are less sensitive than the hanging or zonal pelargonium varieties.

A rustic balcony with the semi-pendent cultivar "Schöne von Grenchen" and the hanging pelargonium "Galilee".

Pelargoniums for patios and balconies

1 "Rio"

Flower: single. **Colour:** light pink, becoming darker towards the centre, with dark red markings. **Inflorescence:** umbel with 10-15 single flowers. **Leaf:** large, dark green with slightly wavy edges. **Growth:** upright, compact. **Note:** a recent variety with unusual flowers, blooms very abundantly and is weather-resistant, suitable for indoors, balcony or garden.

2 "Casino"

Flower: very large, double flower. **Colour:** dark salmon pink, silvery undersides to petals. **Inflorescence:** large umbel with up to 20 individual flowers. **Leaf:** large, light green with a light brown "girdle" marking on the leaf, slightly wavy edges. **Growth:** upright, vigorous growth, branches well. **Note:** will thrive well indoors, on balconies and patios and in the garden (also in flowerbeds).

3 "Champagne"

Flower: large, single flower. **Colour:** light salmon pink with white centre. **Inflorescence:** umbel with 10-20 single individual flowers, early flowering, abundant. **Leaf:** light green with light brown leaf ring, slightly lobed edges. **Growth:** upright, compact, branches well. **Note:** attractive variety which looks good against a darker background. Suitable for indoors, balconies, patios and the garden.

4 "Fidelio"

Flower: large, double individual flowers. **Colour:** pinkish-red. **Inflorescence:** umbel with 15-20 individual flowers. **Leaf:** large, deep green, faint light brown leaf ring. **Growth:** upright, vigorous growth. **Note:** very early flowering variety, weather-hardy, suitable for indoors, balconies, patios and garden (even in flowerbeds).

5 "Flirtpel"

Flower: large, semi-double individual flowers. **Colour:** glowing pink, turning lighter towards the centre, with fine dark red markings. **Inflorescence:** umbels with 10-15 individual flowers. **Leaf:** small, without markings, edges slightly lobed. **Growth:** upright, compact. **Note:** early-flowering balcony, container and bedding pelargonium, needs lots of feeding.

6 "Kardinal"

Flower: very large, single individual flowers. **Colour:** dark lilac, centre of flower violet, orange or scarlet. **Inflorescence:** very large umbels with 15-20 individual flowers. **Leaf:** large, dark green, faintly recognizable leaf ring, slightly lobed edge. **Growth:** upright, very vigorous growth. **Note:** suitable for indoors, balconies, patios and the garden (in containers or flowerbeds), will tolerate semi-shady positions.

7 "Bolero"

Flower: large, double individual flowers. **Colour:** glowing red. **Inflorescence:** umbels with 15-25 separate flowers. **Leaf:** dark green, slightly wavy edge. **Growth:** upright, branches quickly. **Note:** weather-resistant, early-flowering, for indoors, balconies, patios and gardens.

8 "Cabaret"

Flower: large, semi-double individual flowers. **Colour:** glowing salmon pink to orange red, silvery undersides to petals. **Inflorescence:** large umbels with 15-20 individual flowers. **Growth:** upright, branches very quickly. **Leaf:** dark green, lobed edge. **Note:** the withered petals do not fall off; suitable for indoors, balconies, patios and gardens.

9 "Stadt Bern"

Flower: small, single flowers. **Colour:** brilliant red. **Inflorescence:** umbels with 10-15 individual flowers. **Leaf:** small, dark green with black leaf ring. **Growth:** upright. **Note:** will tolerate semi-shade, suitable for indoors, balconies, patios and gardens.

Zonal pelargoniums

1 "Rio"

2 "Casino"

3 "Champagne"

4 "Fidelio"

5 "Flirtpel"

6 "Kardinal"

7 "Bolero"

8 "Cabaret"

9 "Stadt Bern"

Pelargoniums for patios and balconies

1 "Amethyst"

Flower: large, semi-double individual flowers. **Colour:** dark lilac with black markings in the centre, the undersides of the petals are silvery. **Inflorescence:** umbels with 4-10 individual flowers. **Leaf:** dark green, fleshy, smooth on top, lobed edges. **Growth:** compact, short, hanging shoots. **Note:** very popular variety for balconies, containers and mixed groups of plants, will stay compact even in a flowerbox.

2 "Solidor"

Flower: very large, semi-double, individual flowers. **Colour:** light salmon pink with dark red eye. **Inflorescence:** umbels with 5-10 individual flowers, very abundantly flowering. **Leaf:** light green, fleshy, smooth upsides, edges with pointed lobes. **Growth:** very weather-resistant, suitable for many uses (for example, containers, balcony boxes, etc).

3 "Feuercascade"

Flower: single. **Colour:** fire red with fine, dark red markings. **Inflorescence:** umbels with 3-12 individual flowers. **Leaf:** small, dark green, edges with pointed lobes. **Growth:** hanging, very vigorously growing (up to 1.5 m per year/5 ft). **Note:** weather-resistant, "self-tidying", universally suitable for balconies, walls, baskets, large containers, requires lots of fertilizer. **NB:** often sold under the name of "Balkon Imperial".

4 "Ville de Paris"

Flower: single. **Colour:** dark red markings on a lighter red background, which may grow a little paler in very sunny positions. **Inflorescence:** umbels with 2-8 individual flowers. **Leaf:** medium sized, with smooth upperside, edges strongly lobed. **Growth:** hanging, very vigorously growing (up to 1.5 m/5 ft per year). **Note:** ancestor of all cascade varieties; suitable for all sites. **NB:** needs lots of feeding.

5 "Schöne von Grenchen"

Flower: large, semi-double, individual flowers. **Colour:** warm, brilliant shade of red. **Inflorescence:** umbels with 3-10 individual flowers. **Leaf:** medium-sized to large, light green, lobed edges. **Growth:** semi-pendent (a cross between upright and hanging pelargoniums), compact growth. **Note:** well-known variety, weather-resistant, relatively resistant to diseases, easy to propagate, good for overwintering.

6 "Sugar Baby"

Flower: miniature to small individual flowers, double flowering. **Colour:** light pink. **Inflorescence:** umbels with 4-10 individual flowers. **Leaf:** medium sized, light green, fleshy, smooth, with 5 segments. **Growth:** hanging, medium vigorous growth. **Note:** attractive pot variety, also for baskets, basins and individual planting, masses of buds; slightly sensitive to weather conditions.

7 "Mexikanerin"

Flower: very large, double flowers. **Colour:** white with red edges and red markings in the centres. **Inflorescence:** umbels with 3-6 individual flowers. **Leaf:** medium-sized, lobed edges, faintly visible leaf ring. **Growth:** hanging. **Note:** early flowering, will thrive in semi-shady position too; especially suitable for baskets and balcony boxes.

8 "Tavira"

Flower: large, double flowers with slightly wavy petals. **Colour:** brilliant red. **Inflorescence:** umbels with 3-6 flowers. **Leaf:** medium-sized, lobed edges. **Growth:** hanging, vigorously growing. **Note:** very weather-resistant variety, suitable for balcony boxes, containers and mixed groups of plants.

9 "Galilee"

Flower: medium-sized, semi-double flowers: **Colour:** light pink becoming darker towards the centre, with silvery undersides. **Inflorescence:** umbels with 2-6 individual flowers, profusely blooming. **Leaf:** small, dark green, fleshy, smooth upperside, edges very lobed. **Growth:** hanging, long shoots. **Note:** suitable for balcony boxes and containers, goes well with upright red pelargoniums, easy to overwinter.

Hanging and semi-pendent pelargoniums

1 "Amethyst"

2 "Solidor"

3 "Feuercascade"

4 "Ville de Paris"

5 "Schöne von Grenchen"

6 "Sugar Baby"

7 "Mexikanerin"

8 "Tavira"

9 "Galilee"

Indoor pelargoniums

This section deals with varieties of pelargoniums that are especially easy to care for indoors.
● Scented-leaved and wild pelargoniums (see pp. 24, 52, 53) with an unusual beauty of their own, which are presently being rediscovered by more and more pelargonium enthusiasts.
● Varieties of pelargoniums that were popular in our grandmothers' day (see pp. 54, 55).
● The charming fancy-leaved pelargoniums (see pp. 56, 57), nearly all of which have flowers as well as leaves and which will thrive outdoors as well as indoors.

Scented-leaved and wild pelargoniums

Many scented-leaved pelargoniums are wild pelargoniums which exist in the same form in South Africa to this day. Some of them are even used in the manufacture of perfumes. Some scented-leaved pelargoniums (see pp. 52, 53, Nos 5, 8, 9), however, are hybrids, bred from crosses between various wild pelargoniums.

Appearance
Photographs of their leaves (see p. 24) and flowers (see p. 53) help to demonstrate just how varied the charming scented-leaved and wild pelargoniums can be.

Tips on care
Position: Light and airy; provide shade in the summer when the sunlight is very intense.
Watering: moderate (see p. 23).
Soil: water-permeable; for example, a mixture of standard potting compost with lots of sand (see p. 25).

Feeding: with liquid compound fertilizer in water; during the summer, half of the recommended dose every two weeks; stop feeding entirely during the second month of winter (see p. 25).
Overwintering: in the cool period (5° C/41° F) of four to six weeks during the second and third months of winter; do not water or feed during this period, only spray lightly (see p. 31).
Pests: white fly. Control (see p. 27).

Regal pelargoniums

Pelargonium grandiflorum hybrids were created by crossing *Pelargonium cucullatum* (still used today as a hedging plant in Capetown) with other wild pelargoniums. Also called English or indoor pelargoniums.

Appearance
Regal pelargoniums are very compact-growing plants, which have flowers that tend to grow, most attractively, in the centre of the plant, surrounded by leaves. The individual flowers are very large and grow in umbels. Their colours range from almost blackish-purple to briliant red and pastel shades of red to white (see p. 55).

Tips on care
Position: a light, airy windowsill; provide shade in the summer if the sun is very hot.
Watering: very sparingly (p. 23).
Soil: very water-permeable and nutrient-rich, for example, a mixture of standard potting compost and sand (see p. 25).
Feeding: once a week in summer with "flowering" fertilizer in water; stop completely during the second

winter month (see p. 25).
Overwintering: as for scented-leaved and wild pelargoniums (see p. 31).
Pests: rare; white fly. Control see p. 27.

Fancy-leaved pelargoniums

Fancy-leaved pelargoniums are cultivars of zonal pelargoniums with especially interesting, colourful leaves (see p. 44). They were created by multiple crosses and mutations.

Appearance
Strikingly coloured, variable-edged leaves (see p. 57). The flowers are usually smaller than those of other zonal hybrids and will only develop properly in a very sunny position.

Tips on care
Position: full sun.
Watering: sparingly, as for zonal pelargoniums (see p. 23).
Soil: water-permeable and nutrient-rich; for example, a mixture of standard potting compost and sand (see p. 25).
Feeding: once a week in summer with liquid compound fertilizer in water; stop completely in early autumn (see p. 25).
Overwintering: as for zonal pelargoniums (see p. 29).
Pests: rare (see diseases, p. 26).

Scented-leaved pelargonium "Scarlet Pet"
This scented-leaved pelargonium is a cultivated hybrid with leaves that release the delicate aroma of oranges.

Indoor pelargoniums

1 Scarlet pelargonium
Pelargonium inquinans

Flower: single flowers, almost round. **Colour:** intense scarlet (in exceptional cases also pale pink or even white flowers). **Inflorescence:** umbels with 5-30 individual flowers. **Leaf:** dark green, hairy uppersides, heart-shaped markings at base of stalk, lobed edges. **Growth:** upright, 1-2 m high (40-80 in). **Scent:** strong. **Note:** already cultivated in Britain by 1714.

2 Scented pelargonium
Pelargonium fragrans

Flower: single flowers with very delicate petals. **Colour:** white with fine reddish lines. **Inflorescence:** umbels with 10-25 individual flowers. **Leaf:** tiny, heart-shaped leaflets on long stalks; leaves have lobed edges and are slightly wavy. **Growth:** delicate. **Scent:** when touched, strong smell of pine essence. **Note:** attractive indoor plant, easy to care for.

3 Myrrh-leaved pelargonium
Pelargonium myrrhifolium

Flower: very dainty. **Colour:** delicate pink, upper petals have purple flamed stripes. **Inflorescence:** umbels with 2-6 individual flowers. **Leaf:** fine, feathery, hairy. **Growth:** shrub-like, up to 40 cm high (16 in). **Note:** will flower nearly all year round, loves sandy soil.

4 Almond-scented pelargonium
Pelargonium blandfordianum

Flower: single, delicate flowers, 1-2 cm (under ½ in-¾ in). **Colour:** white, red style and stigma, upper petals have dark pink markings. **Inflorescence:** umbels with 2-4 individual flowers. **Leaf:** delicate, feathery, shiny grey green. **Growth:** dainty. **Scent:** pleasant smell of almonds; the scent may vary at times to smell more like sage or wormwood. **Note:** very suitable for indoors.

5 "Els"
(Pelargonium – Stellar hybrid)

Flower: star-shaped, up to 10 fine, pointed petals arranged in a circle. **Colour:** dark salmon pink. **Inflorescence:** umbels with 3-10 individual flowers. **Leaf:** star-shaped, soft hairs. **Growth:** remains small. **Scent:** strong.
Note: this scented-leaved pelargonium belongs to the group of stellar hybrids which possess star-shaped leaves and flowers and are especially suitable for indoors.

6 Wood-sorrel-leaved pelargonium
Pelargonium acetosum

Flower: fine, delicate, narrow petals. **Colour:** salmon pink to white. **Inflorescence:** umbels with 2-7 individual flowers. **Leaf:** upside-down, oval, blue green, fleshy, very lobed edges and slightly tinged with red. **Growth:** bushy, well-branched, small shrub, up to 60 cm (2 ft) high, sparse foliage. **Scent:** faint. **Note:** very suitable for indoors.

7 "Prince of Orange"
(hybrid)

Flower: single flower, up to 3 cm (just over 1 in). **Colour:** light pink with fine, dark red markings. **Inflorescence:** umbel with 1-2 flowers. **Leaf:** small, slightly curled and slashed edges. **Growth:** upright, up to 30 cm (12 in) high. **Scent:** smell of oranges. **Note:** a pleasantly scented hybrid that is easy to propagate.

8 Gout pelargonium
Pelargonium gibbosum

Flower: fine, slightly recurved, small petals on long stalks. **Colour:** ocre yellow to greenish-yellow. Inflorescence: umbels with 6-14 flowers. **Leaf:** blue green, divided, very fleshy. **Growth:** climbing, swollen nodes on the stalks (hence the name!), up to 2 m high (80 in). **Scent:** flowers smell strongly of musk at night. **Note:** the scent is released after sunset to attract moths for pollination.

9 "Scarlet Pet"
(hybrid)

Flower: dainty. **Colour:** brilliant red. **Inflorescence:** umbels with 3-8 flowers. **Leaf:** medium-sized, dark green, slit edges. **Growth:** vigorously growing, hairy stems. **Scent:** smells of balm and oranges. **Note:** a fast-growing, profusely flowering pelargonium hybrid that is easy to propagate.

Scented-leaved and wild pelargoniums

1 *Pelargonium inquinans*

2 *Pelargonium fragrans*

3 *Pelargonium myrrhifolium*

4 *Pelargonium blandfordianum*

5 *"Els"*

6 *Pelargonium acetosum*

7 *"Prince of Orange"*

8 *Pelargonium gibbosum*

9 *"Scarlet Pet"*

53

Indoor pelargoniums

1 "Jupiter"

Flower: large, single, individual flowers. **Colour:** shades of lilac, stronger dark lilac markings, clearly visible patch of the same colour on the two upper petals. **Inflorescence:** umbels with 4-10 individual flowers. **Leaf:** medium-sized, almost circular, serrated edges. **Growth:** fairly vigorous, upright. *Note:* ideal pelargonium for indoors.

2 "Mickey"

Flower: medium-sized, single. **Colour:** mainly violet; the two upper petals have an extensive blackish-purple marking and the three lower petals a blackish-purple dot. **Inflorescence:** umbels with 4-8 individual flowers. **Leaf:** five segments, finely serrated edge. **Flower:** medium-fast-growing. *Note:* an unusual variety, branches well.

3 "Mikado"

Flower: large, wavy petals, edges of petals turning out. **Colour:** dark salmon pink with a dark red patch on each petal. **Inflorescence:** dense umbels with 6-8 individual flowers. **Leaf:** heart-shaped with 3-5 segments and clearly serrated edges. **Growth:** medium-fast-growing, the flowers are close above the leaves. *Note:* flowers very profusely.

4 "Muttertag"

Flower: large, almost round petals, arranged in a circle. **Colour:** orange red with dark red markings on the two upper petals and white ones on the three lower petals, all finely edged in white. **Inflorescence:** umbels with 2-6 individual flowers. **Leaf:** small, lobed, with serrated edges. **Growth:** medium-fast-growing. *Note:* very striking markings on flowers.

5 "Jasmin"

Flower: large individual flowers, petals slightly wavy towards the edges. **Colour:** pure white with fine purple violet markings on the two upper petals. **Inflorescence:** loose umbels with 2-6 individual flowers. **Leaf:** heart-shaped and round with a serrated edge. **Growth:** fast-growing. *Note:* flowers profusely.

6 "Frühlingsgruss"

Flower: large individual flowers with a slightly wavy edge. **Colour:** delicate pink with a large purple-red marking on the two upper petals, while the three lower petals have fine purple rays. **Inflorescence:** umbels with 4-8 individual flowers. **Leaf:** 5 segments with very serrated edges. **Growth:** medium-fast-growing. *Note:* flowers profusely.

7 "Silvia"

Flower: slightly wavy petals. **Colour:** brilliant red with dark red markings on the two upper petals. **Inflorescence:** loose umbels with 4-6 individual flowers. **Leaf:** heart-shaped with serrated edge. **Growth:** medium-fast-growing. *Note:* do not place in strong sunlight!

8 "Göttweig"

Flower: very large single flowers, petals slightly wavy. **Colour:** salmon pink, upper petals tinged dark red with dark veins, lighter centre. **Inflorescence:** loose umbels with 2-6 individual flowers. **Leaf:** large, slightly lobed, 3-4 segments, dentate. **Growth:** fast-growing. *Note:* flowers profusely.

9 "Valentin"

Flower: large single flowers with almost round, smooth petals, which are arranged in a circle. **Colour:** brilliant violet with dark violet markings on the two upper petals, lighter centre. **Inflorescence:** loose umbels with 2-4 individual flowers. **Leaf:** large, divided into 3 segments, serrated edges. **Growth:** fast-growing. *Note:* flowers profusely.

Regal pelargoniums

1 *"Jupiter"*

2 *"Mickey"*

3 *"Mikado"*

4 *"Muttertag"*

5 *"Jasmin"*

6 *"Frühlingsgruss"*

7 *"Silvia"*

8 *"Göttweig"*

9 *"Valentin"*

Indoor pelargoniums

1 "Pink Golden Harry Hieouver"

Flower: single, medium sized. **Colour:** salmon pink. **Inflorescence:** umbels with with 5-15 individual flowers. **Shape of leaf:** very large, slightly lobed, hairy. **Colour of leaf:** light green basic colour, partly golden yellow, wide leaf ring turning lighter towards the outer edge. **Growth:** upright, fast growing. **Note:** suitable for all positions.

2 "The Czar"

Flower: single. **Colour of flower:** carmine red. **Inflorescence:** umbels with 7-10 individual flowers. **Shape of leaf:** medium-sized, slightly lobed. **Colour of leaf:** basic light green, dark brown, very broad leaf ring. **Growth:** upright, medium-fast-growing. **Note:** suitable for all positions.

3 "The Boar"

Flower: single. **Colour of flower:** salmon pink. **Inflorescence:** 5-10 individual flowers. **Shape of leaf:** almost round, slightly lobed. **Colour of leaf:** light green, brownish-black centre, coloured along veins. **Growth:** upright, fast-growing, but delicate. **Note:** suitable for indoors.

4 "Masterpiece"

Flower: small, semi-double. **Colour of flower:** light orange. **Inflorescence:** umbels with 5-10 individual flowers. **Shape of leaf:** large, slightly lobed. **Colour of leaf:** dark green centre, blackish leaf ring very visible, outer edge creamy white with traces of red. **Growth:** upright, fast-growing. **Note:** suitable for all positions, easy to propagate.

5 "Miss Burdett-Coutts"

Flower: single. **Colour:** light red. **Inflorescence:** umbels with 5-10 individual flowers. **Shape of leaf:** very small, lobed. **Colour of leaf:** multi-coloured, green centre, dark brown leaf ring, wine red overlying colour, rippled, narrow white edge. **Growth:** upright, slow-growing. **Note:** very suitable for indoors.

6 "Dolly Vardon"

Flower: single. **Colour:** light red. **Inflorescence:** umbels with 7-15 individual flowers. **Shape of leaf:** small leaf, slightly lobed edge. **Colour of leaf:** multi-coloured, dark green centre, almost black leaf ring, bright red overlay, rippled, narrow, cream outer edge. **Growth:** medium-fast-growing. **Note:** very suitable for indoors.

7 "Bird Dancer"

Flower: single, star-shaped. **Colour:** salmon pink with irregular white circles. **Inflorescence:** umbels with 5-10 individual flowers. **Shape of leaf:** small, star-shaped, tapering leaf segments. **Colour of leaf:** dark green, blackish-brown ring, green tips. **Growth:** small flowers, compact growth. **Note:** very suitable for indoors, stellar hybrid (= star-shaped leaves or star-shaped flowers).

8 "Madame Salleron"

Exception: no flowers are formed. **Shape of leaf:** small to medium-sized leaves, almost completely round, upperside slightly convex, slightly wavy edges. **Colour of leaf:** greyish-green basic colour, white edge of varying widths, no leaf ring visible. **Growth:** upright, medium-fast-growing. **Note:** popular variety for decorating graves, known since 1877.

9 "Freak of Nature"

Exception: no flowers are formed. **Shape of leaf:** medium sized leaves, edges wavy and holed, lobed. **Colour of leaf:** light cream centre, extending more or less to the edges, edges green. **Growth:** upright, fast-growing. **Note:** difficult to propagate because of its chlorophyll deficiency.

Fancy-leaved pelargoniums

1 *"Pink Golden Harry Hieouver"*

2 *"The Czar"*

3 *"The Boar"*

4 *"Masterpiece"*

5 *"Miss Burdett-Coutts"*

6 *"Dolly Vardon"*

7 *"Bird Dancer"*

8 *"Madame Salleron"*

9 *"Freak of Nature"*

Geraniums in the garden

Geraniums are hardy shrubs which are sometimes called "stork's bill" although *Geranium* really means "crane's bill" (see p. 8).

Geraniums are used in plantings of mixed shrubs, rock gardens, in wild gardens and in wild flower gardens. Low-growing species are useful for their ground-covering properties and for covering large expanses between shrubs that grow taller.

These undemanding plants flower from late spring to late summer and love chalky, nutrient-rich soils which may also include a little clay. You can buy them in large plastic containers at garden centres and nurseries, etc. from early spring to late autumn. Plants bought in spring should have already put out all their shoots. They will flower during the first year after planting. In the autumn, when the parts of

the plant above ground have turned brown, cut off the stalks about 20 cm (8 in) above the soil. Do not cut them back too early, as they turn a lovely shade of red in the autumn. Winter protection will not be necessary. The simplest method of propagating is division of the rootstock in the spring (see propagating by division, p. 38). Propagating with seed is possible but time-comsuming.

A wild garden with a harmoniously balanced plant community, comprising geraniums, grasses, Aruncus and saxifrage.

Geraniums in the garden

Tall crane's bill
Geranium macrorrhizum
Flower: pink, "Spessart" is blue violet, "Ingversson" deep pink.
Flowering time: late spring to late summer. **Growth:** up to 1 m (40 in), large bushes.

Caucasian crane's bill
Geranium platypetalum
Flower: large flowers, light violet with beautiful markings.
Flowering time: early to late summer. **Growth:** up to 80 cm (32 in), vigorous growth.

Dalmatian crane's bill
Geranium dalmaticum
Flower: pink, "Album" is pure white.
Flowering time: early to late summer. **Growth:** up to 10 cm (4 In), large cushions.

French crane's bill
Geranium endressi
Flower: bright pure pink.
Flowering time: late spring to early autumn. **Growth:** up to 30 cm (1 ft) large bushes.

Dwarf crane's bill
Geranium subcaulescens
Flower: carmine red with darker centre. **Flowering time:** early to mid-summer. **Growth:** creeps.

Bloody crane's bill
Geranium sanguineum
Flower: reddish-violet. **Flowering time:** early summer to early autumn. **Growth:** up to 30 cm (1 ft), ground-covering.

Meebold's crane's bill
Geranium meeboldii
Flower: blue violet with wine-red markings. **Flowering time:** early summer to early autumn. **Growth:** up to 30 cm (1 ft), large bushes.

△ The Armenian crane's bill (Geranium psylosteum) flowers in mid-summer.
▽ The flowers of Geranium grandiflorum may be 4 cm (1½ in) across.

Index

Figures given in bold indicate illustrations.

Index

nettle brew 27
nodes **23**, 30
NPK ratio 15
nutrient deficiency, symptoms of 23
nutrients 12, 22, 23, 45
  absorbing of 23

oedema 26
organic (biological) fertilizer 15
organic-mineral basic fertilizer 16
  compound fertilizer 15, 16, 25
overwintering 28, 40, 42, 43, 44, 45, 50
  in a bag 30
  in a warm room 31
  in paper 31
  rules of 29
  space-saving 31

parasites 23
parent plant 35
peat 12, 14
  dark 12
  pellets 33, 35
  propagating pots 34, 35
pedestals 52, 53
pelargonium, hanging 7, **17**, 20, 28, **37**,
  40, 42, **43**, 44, **45**, **49**
  in balcony boxes **17**
  in hanging baskets **17**
  indoors 11, 18, 23, 26, 31, 36, 43, 50,
  52, **54**, **56**
  large-flowering 43
  scarlet 52
  "self-tidying" 39, 44
  shield 44
  semi-pendent 7, 44, 45, **45**, **49**
species:
  Pelargonium 8
    acetosum 52, **53**
    blandfordianum 52, **53**
    capitatum 37
    cucullatum 7, 50
    cunanifolium 37
    fragrans 37, 52, **53**
    gibbosum 37, 52, **53**
    glutinosum 24, **24**
    grandiflorum 43
    Grandiflorum hybrids 7, 50
    graveolens 8, 24, **24**

    inquinans 6, 44, 52, **53**
    myrrhifolium 52, 53
    odoratissimum 24, **24**
    papilonaceum 37
    peltatum 7, 44
    Peltatum hybrids 7, 44
    quercifolium 24, **24**
    radens 8, 24, **24**
    tomentosum 24, **24**, 37
    viscosissimum 24, **24**
    Zonal hybrids 6, 44
    x *Peltatum* hybrids 7, 44
varieties:
  "Amethyst" 48, **49**
  "Balkon Imperial" 48
  "Bern" **38**
  "Bird Dancer" 56, **57**
  "Bolero" 46, **47**
  "Caberet" 46, **47**
  "Casino" **14**, 46, **47**
  "Champagne" 46, **47**
  "Chelsea Gem" **cover**, **10**
  "Countess of Scarborough" 37
  "Dolly Vardon" 56, **57**
  "Els" 52, **53**
  "Feuercascade" **19**, 44, 48, **49**
  "Fidelio" 46, **47**
  "Flirtpel" 46, **47**
  "Freak of Nature" 56, **57**
  "Frühlingsgruss" 54, **55**
  "Galilee" **40**, 48, 49
  "Göttweig" 54, **55**
  "Jasmin" 54, **55**
  "Joy Lucile" **24**
  "Jupiter" 54, **55**
  "Kardinal" **14**, 46, **47**
  "Lachscascade" 44
  "Lila-Mini-Cascade" 44
  "Madame Salleron" 56, **57**
  "Mexikanerin" 48, **49**
  "Mickey" 54, **55**
  "Mikado" 54, **55**
  "Miss Burdett Coutts" 56, **57**
  "Muttertag" 54, **55**
  "Prince of Orange" 52, **53**
  "Princess Anne" 37, 43
  "Scarlet Pet" **51**, 52, **53**
  "Pink Golden Harry Hieouver" 56, **57**
  "Rio" 46, **47**

  "Rote-Mini-Cascade" 44
  "Schöne von Grenchen" **cover**, **33**, **45**,
  48, 49
  "Silvia" 54, **55**
  "Solidor" 48, **49**
  "Stadt Bern" 46, **47**
  "Sugar Baby" 48, **49**
  "Tavira" 48, **49**
  "The Boar" 56, **57**
  "The Czar" 56, **57**
  "Valentin" 54, **55**
  "Ville de Paris" 44, 48, **49**
  "Virginia" **cover**, **20**
  "White Unique" **24**
pelargoniums, zonal 6, **14**, **17**, 20, 28, 40,
  42, 44, 47, **47**
pergola 39
Perlite 31
pests 39, 42
petals 44
pinching out 30
planting 18, 19, 38, 39, 40
plants, accompanying 39
  annual 28, 42, 43
  combinations of **17**, 39, 42, 43, **43**, 44,
  45
  for containers 19
  fully grown 10
  half-grown 10
  indoor 52, 56
  pruning 43
plastic pots 32, 34, 35, 36
polythene hoods 23
position 12, **13**, 18, 19, 38, 45, 50
pot, propagating 12, 18
  holders 19
potting 18, **18**
  compost 13, 20, 25
  pricking out 34, 35, 38
propagating 32
  by division 38
  from cuttings 35, 37
  from seed 32, 37, 38
  methods 36
protection from wind 25
  in winter 58
pruning 25, 30, **30**, 40, 42
  accompanying plants 43

Index

Cover photographs:
Front cover: *semi-pendent pelargonium
"Schöne von Grenchen";*
Inside front cover: *hanging cascade vari-
eties;*
Inside back cover: *a luxuriant display of
hanging and zonal pelargoniums;*
Back cover: *ivy-leaved pelargonium
"Chelsea Gem" (top), regal pelargoni-
ums (below).*

Photographic acknowledgements:
Altmanns: page 9; *Burda*/Mein schöner
Garten: page 41; Reinhard: inside back
cover; Schmidt-Thomé: pages 5, 17,
63; Silvestris/Riedmiller: pages 14, 57
(3, 6, 8, 9); Skogstad: pages 13, 43, 61.
Riedmiller: all other photographs.

This edition published 1994 by
Merehurst Limited
Ferry House, 51-57 Lacy Road,
Putney, London SW15 1PR
Reprinted 1995 (three times)

© 1989 Gräfe und Unzer GmbH, Munich

ISBN 1 85391 391 X

A catalogue record for this book is available from the British Library.

English text copyright ©
Merehurst Limited 1995
Translated by Astrid Mick
Edited by Lesley Young
Design and typesetting by Paul Cooper
Printed in Hong Kong by Wing King Tong